The Daily Seed

Inspiring Words to Plant, Cultivate and Nurture Your Growth

Sheila Whittington

FINN-PHYLLIS
PRESS

Published by Finn-Phyllis Press, Inc.

Cover design by JetLaunch.net

Edited by Elizabeth Lyons

The Daily Seed / Sheila Whittington —— 1st ed.

ISBN 978-1-7344043-0-2 (pbk)
ISBN 978-1-7344043-1-9 (eBook)

Dedicated to all of you who, in your desire to grow and live your best life, are open to receiving the wisdom of the Universe without expectation of how it will be delivered. Also, to Brent, Blake, and Aiden for being my most faithful and loving deliverymen.

"There is a seed inside of every tree and a tree inside of every seed."

—MATSHONA DHLIWAYO

INTRODUCTION

I n 2013, a client and good friend of mine encouraged me to teach a course for women struggling with depleted self-worth, lack of clarity and direction, indecision, and feeling stuck due to all the rules, shoulds, and shouldn'ts in their lives. I agreed and put together a six-week course that I called "Core Living." I wanted to help them in a way that would feel safe, give them absolute permission to be who they are and provide a supportive community to prove that they were not alone. We worked in six core areas: relationships/family, career/work, physical health, time, money, and spirituality. The experience was truly life-changing for all of us.

In an effort to keep them engaged between in-person sessions, I started sending a daily email that contained a bit of wisdom and encouragement. I called it The Daily Seed. Every morning, I would sit down, ground myself, connect with the Universe, and ask, "What do they need today?" I would then simply listen. A message or tidbit would come, and I'd type it up in a way that was inviting and easy to consider. I then sent it off to this small group.

Nearly every day I received a response from one of the participants, wondering, "How did you know that was exactly what I needed today?!" They started telling others about The Daily Seed, and I continued adding new readers to the list as well as Tweeting out the messages in the event that they might be helpful to anyone else. That was in 2013, and I am still connecting with the Universe every morning, Monday through Friday, and sending out new Daily Seeds.

During the past six years, I've had many requests from clients and email readers to put my Daily Seeds into a collection where they can be referred to more easily. They're written in a very casual, easy-to-process way that often includes humor, irony, and metaphor. This book provides an assortment of favorite Daily Seeds.

Did I write this book expecting it to change the world? Of course not. I write each Daily Seed with the invitation and hope that its reader will find a bit of wisdom, love, and encouragement to make choices that feel right and true for them.

When that happens, the world changes.

Applying The Daily Seeds

A bed of raw dirt can be transformed into a garden of beauty and abundance when the right seeds are planted, cultivated, and nurtured. Each seed in this book is an offering of wisdom, written with an intention to fertilize and enrich your personal growth in a way that will inspire you to blossom and thrive.

The seeds have been arranged in random order so that you can either read the book from front to back or just open up to a page and discover the message that shows up for you. Each seed has also been categorized. A symbol representing the seed's primary topic has been included at the end of each to help you better navigate your journey with the book, especially when you're seeking help in a specific area. Simply refer to the Index at the back of the book, and it will guide you to the page(s) you are most in need of at any given moment.

You will, however, find that several seeds provide subtle guidance in more than one category, so I invite you to explore them all.

Personal Power seeds will help you stand up for yourself and feel your deep inner worth.

 Thoughts to Ponder seeds will give you an opportunity to recognize what is true for you.

 Lessons seeds are the "instantly applicable" and often "take action now" seeds.

 Perspective seeds give you an opportunity to consider things from a different angle.

 Intention seeds help you set a course for what you want and determine how to follow it.

 Opportunity seeds are offerings from the Universe to help you expand and grow.

 Choice seeds encompass the concept of free will, personal power, boundaries, and consequences—both positive and negative.

 Fear seeds explore the negative emotions that inhibit you from being, doing, or having what you want and from truly loving yourself. They also assist you in navigating fear's affects.

The Daily Seed

It's been said that "our deepest, darkest fear is not that something negative will happen, but rather that we won't be able to handle it."

So, how do you relax from THAT fear?

One approach is to recall all the things you've been afraid of so far that *haven't* resulted in a situation you weren't able to handle. Of course you handled them—you are still here! Life has continued. Time has passed. You have grown stronger and wiser.

My hunch is that you will have the fear of *not being able to handle it* again (more than once). The fear may not be easy or pleasant. It may even be incredibly painful at times. But, handle it you will, because that's what you do. You have evidence that this is true. 😮

Don't you feel silly when, after sitting in anguish wondering why you're not getting what you want, you suddenly realize that you forgot to ask for it?

Silly you. Silly me. Silly us.

Are you asking for what you want?

Just ask. ⊚

This is what fear is: an emotion, a feeling, an energy that we take on in our bodies, minds, and hearts. Fear can be very powerful.

This is what fear is NOT: a physical barrier, a physical roadblock, a physical weapon being held to your head.

Fear has only as much power as you give it. It can only stop you if you let it. Why would you choose to do that? The answer is that you are giving more power to fear than you are giving love and strength to yourself. 😲

You can be intelligent but not wise.
You can be wise but not intelligent.
You can also be both.
But neither determines your worth.

"Hope for the best and prepare for the worst" means
have a positive attitude, but be prepared for disaster.

If you are preparing for disaster more diligently than you are
at keeping your attitude positive, what do you think you're
going to end up with? The Universe is going to deliver
whatever it is you are vibrating most strongly.

Since that's the case, if you're going to hope for the best, why
not also be prepared for the best?

"I had/have no choice" is a lie, whether you say it to yourself or to others. You always have a choice. Always.

The likely reason why you feel you have no choice is that you are uncomfortable with the anticipated consequence of your choice. Perhaps you fear your choice will bring confrontation, debt, loneliness, or rejection. Maybe it will. Maybe it won't.

The minute you tell yourself, "I have no choice," you give up your power. However, if you'll be brave enough to say, "I choose this because I am afraid," you at least retain and realize your power to choose. You do not render yourself powerless. You admit you are afraid—but not powerless. And you can gather the courage to choose again.

Choice is power. You hold the power to change your life.

Power to the people.

Our humanness WANTS to be happy. It is our mission and our goal. It is what our heart yearns for.

How often do you wake up and set an intention to feel sick or uncomfortable or tired or angry or lonely or worried? When you're happy, how often do you say to yourself, "I wish I felt crappy right now?"

Happiness is one breath away. A smile away. A laugh away. A hug away. A love away. I invite you to set an intention to feel and appreciate more happy moments today—and every day. It's what your heart and soul long for. Watch what happens.

More happy. Less crappy. ◎

Expecting or demanding that somebody else does something that you aren't willing to do or that you won't or don't do yourself will most likely present an excellent wake-up call or opportunity for YOU to grow.

Blink. Blink. 🌠

When you are in someone else's business, meaning:

when you are deciding in your mind or expressing aloud what is best for someone else according to your thoughts and beliefs, or when you are trying to control the outcome of somebody else's experience to fit your needs and desires because it would make you feel more comfortable or validated or right...

...who is taking care of your business?

I invite you to remember that everyone has their own path and their own journey. Mistakes will be made. In fact, mistakes MUST be made. Our job is not to control another's journey or protect them from failure. Our job is to love them through their journey while we stay in our own business and love ourselves through our own.

Are you gripped by fear of the unknown? Afraid to make a move because of the terrible "what ifs"? Worried about what might happen or, equally as bad, what might not happen? What an awful but oh-so-common place to put yourself.

Let me offer relief by way of this one thought: it is ALL **unknown**.

This morning before you opened your eyes, did you absolutely know you would be able to see? Before you took your shower, did you absolutely know that water would come out? Before you turned the key in your car's ignition, did you absolutely know it would start? We take these simple things for granted. We assume they will work, and they usually do. We don't lie awake worrying about them. But, in truth, we don't REALLY know they will work. We only trust and have faith that they will.

The Universe/God is always working for your best and highest good. Trust, have faith, and move forward. Believe it or not, you being here right now is proof that it has worked for you so far. 😮

Constant complaining to others with no intention of turning things around is like knowing you have an infectious virus and making an extra effort to cough on everyone you see.

Complaining doesn't make things better. It just spreads negative energy.

Hand me the spiritual Clorox, please. 😮

Have you ever read something or listened to someone and thought to yourself, "Yeah, I've heard this before, it's nothing new"? Then a while later, you read or hear something that's basically the same, but presented in a different way, and you feel like it's the most amazing thing you've ever heard. All of a sudden, it just clicks with you!

This type of thing happens all the time. Why? Because, essentially, there is no new information. There are just different deliveries, different receptors, and different timing.

I invite you to be open to receiving whatever it is you need to hear from wherever you need to hear it in its divine timing. 😮

How many times a day do you hear yourself say, "I don't know"?

I don't know how I'm going to do this.
I don't know who can help me.
I don't know what I want.

I don't know may be part of your everyday language; something your brain tells you when it fears you're going to make a change. It's a phrase you've trained yourself to believe, and it keeps you stuck.

Here's a brain re-train tool that will send your fear packing and let your brain do its work: the next time you hear yourself say "I don't know," change the position of your eyes and ask yourself, "What If I DID know?" Let your brain get curious and solve the challenge. Watch how it looks for creative answers. You may find yourself moving in no time.

You DO know.

How many times have you heard "life is hard"? Ah, but life is really quite simple as long as you follow some very simple instructions:

- Say yes when you mean yes and no when you mean no
- Sleep when you're tired, eat when you're hungry
- Tell your truth
- Be responsible for your own happiness
- Stay in your own business
- Follow your instincts and intuition
- Be kind

That's about it.

Instructions are easy to read. It's the following of them that gets tricky: instead of blaming life when things feel hard, I invite you to simply go back and follow the instructions.

Everything happens for a reason. Scientists call it "cause and effect." Spiritualists call it karma. Whatever you want to call it, I invite you to keep this in mind: you may not know the reason something occurs until long after it does. So, if you can't understand why something is happening when it is happening, just wait. It will all unfold in Divine timing and make sense to you.

And, by the way, most of the wisdom comes in the waiting.
😮

People resist wearing glasses for multiple reasons. It makes them feel unattractive, old, nerdy, uncomfortable, and inconvenienced. They don't want to be judged for the way they look or for their need for help. And even though they absolutely know that glasses would allow them see more clearly and function with more ease, they would rather suffer for their vanity than make the change.

I invite you to take a good look at your life. Do you have the tools to change the way you see and do things but continue to choose to resist? Remember, the choice is always yours.

Yup—another eye-opening metaphor. I can see clearly now.
🡇

There's probably been a time or two in your life when you threw your hands to the air and exclaimed, "I just want a normal life!" Ah, normal. You know...Regular. Standard. Of average intelligence. The usual condition. Mostly predictable. Basically, knowing what's going to happen day after day after day. Not many surprises to celebrate. Not many speed-bump challenges to learn from. Very few chances to experience growth. Just...normal.

Normal always sounds good when you're in the thick of things. It feels good for a while—until yearning for something different sets in. Yearning for something new to experience. Something more exciting or fulfilling. A change. And it will set in.

Instead of wishing for a normal life (as described above), I invite you to consider setting intentions for experiencing less stress, being more deliberate, taking more "me time," getting more rest, or whatever it is that makes you feel grounded and centered. From that state, you're ready to experience whatever comes your way. Then, you can let yearning for something different, exciting, and fulfilling be your normal.

Have you noticed that when you're worried that something is going to be hard or uncomfortable or painful, the time between when it's supposed to happen and when it actually does happen feels hard or uncomfortable or painful?

And, have you noticed that when the something happens and it was easier and more comfortable and less painful than you thought it would be, you have the thought, "Wow. I worried for nothing"?

You were right!

In much easier-to-understand terms: worry is for nothing.

Make it easier.

Without warning, a single word, response, action, or inaction by someone else can set us reeling. We can get ourselves worked into a tizzy faster than water bursts through a fire hose and it can ruin our whole day (or more) if we let it. How do we stop this craziness so we can carry on? Try this:

1. Ask yourself, "What am I making this mean? Am I making it mean something about me? (ie., I'm stupid, I'm not desirable/respectable/capable...you get it.) Am I making it mean something about them? (ie., they're stupid, evil, not desirable/respectable/capable, out-to-hurt-me)."

2. Then ask yourself, "Is what I'm making this mean true?" What are the possibilities? If you determine it's not true, then there's nothing you need to do. Let it roll off your shoulders. If you determine it is true or that there is some truth to it, own your part and make necessary adjustments.

Either way, you will at least slow down the tizzy-making process by asking the questions and be able to gather your wits. 'Cuz tizzies? Ain't nobody got time for that!

We're all too busy for a tizzy.

Nothing stops the progress of fulfilling your dreams faster than the word "can't."

- I can't afford it.
- I can't deal with it.
- I can't find love.
- I can't lose weight.
- I can't get my sh*t together.

The more times you repeat your "can't" story, the more real you make it. You search for evidence to support your "can't" story, and saddest of all, you believe it to be true.

But what if it isn't true? (Hint: it ISN'T!) What if you could look beyond the closed door of "can't" and open yourself up to the possibilities?

Here's one way to do it: every time you hear yourself say (or think) the word "can't" or you feel that "stopped" feeling, ask yourself, "But what if I *could*?" Answer that question in full detail, following each trail of possibility. Visualize what would happen if you could. Dream of who you would be if you could. If you are able to visualize even the most remote possibility, then it surely exists, and your "can't" story is no longer valid.

I know I can.

When you're sitting on a sea of sameness where nothing is happening, sometimes rocking the boat is the best way to get the fish to move.

Yes. Metaphor.

Gone fishing.

Picture yourself happily traveling through the desert. Your destination lies at the beautiful horizon, which is just a few miles ahead. You can see it! Arriving is going to be so great! Then, all of a sudden, the wind kicks up a dust-devil, a herd of galloping horses runs across your path, and a 4-wheel drive truck simultaneously pulls out in front of you, slinging sand like a kid on a playground. What happened to your vision? Where is your beautiful horizon? Where is your sense of direction? Where the heck are you? All you can see is swirling dust; you're completely turned around.

Life feels like that sometimes—out of nowhere. The good news is that, eventually, the dust-devils swirl away, the horses follow their own path, and the speeding truck is but a dot in the distance. Fortunately, all you have to do to get your bearings and be on your happy way is stop and allow the dust to settle. Get a clear vision, center yourself, get back on the road, and head toward that beautiful horizon you've had your eyes on.

Arriving is going to be so great! 🎯

Taking a cake out of the oven too soon will cause it to fall in the middle.

Speeding to an appointment will net you a ticket—or worse, an accident.

Cramming too much into a paper bag will split the sides, rendering it unusable.

And, all that time you think you're saving will be lost to the frustrating inconvenience of the undesired outcome.

If this sounds familiar, I have to ask, what's your hurry? Why so fast? Life is NOT passing you by. You are passing *through* life and not even enjoying it. I invite you to slow down. Be aware of what you're trying to force to happen. Ask yourself, "What will the consequences be if I hurry through this? What am I afraid I will miss if I slow down?" Make friends with time. Have patience for that which you really value.

All timing is Divine. 😮

How can I be more spiritual? Should I:

> • Meditate? (You don't have to, but some people find it helpful.)
> • Go to church? (You don't have to, but some people find it helpful.)
> • Do yoga? chant? burn incense? (You don't have to, but some people find it helpful.)

The answer is, you can't be more spiritual. You already *are* spiritual, just as you already are human. However, you can feel more spiritually connected, and doing so is as easy as taking a moment, clearing your thoughts, breathing deeply, and allowing yourself to simply be who you are without expectation or judgment.

The god-in-you will rock your world if you simply open up and allow.

What does it mean when people say they want work/life balance? Picture it: a scale with work on one side and everything else in their life on the other. Does that mean that work equals half their life? And, if the scale is balanced, doesn't that mean that nothing is moving? Sounds boring and stagnant.

What if we ditched the scale and changed the desire to work/life harmony, where everything we did flowed like the pleasing arrangement of all parts? What if we embraced life as an ever-moving symphony rather than a stagnant scale of measure?

Why take a risk of having your life *hang in the balance* when you can *go with the flow*? There's a lot of happy in harmony.

"Compare and Despair" happens when you measure yourself against someone else and beat yourself up because you believe that you're not as good as they are or haven't accomplished as much as they have. You have a deep feeling of "I should be better." And, not only do you treat *yourself* poorly, sometimes you build animosity toward the person you're comparing yourself to and tear them down to make yourself feel better (which rarely has a lasting feel-good effect and perpetuates negativity). It all feels crappy.

So, what do you do to get out of Compare and Despair?

What if, instead of *beating* yourself up, you used them as **inspiration** to *build* yourself up? After all, if they already have it, then the possibility exists for you to have it as well. If they did it, then the possibility exists for you to do it. The Universe is abundant. The possibilities are endless. Allow yourself to be inspired by others to explore the possibilities and get what you want!

There's room beyond compare for all of us.

FEAR is the F-word that stops us when making a change is too uncomfortable to face. **FAITH** is the F-word that allows us to move when ***NOT*** making a change is too uncomfortable to face.

FAITH. The acceptable F-word every time.

Drop the bomb. 😮

Sometimes, the easiest way to end an argument, disagreement, or plain old nagging is to calmly utter these four words to your assailant:

"You could be right."

Then move on. It doesn't mean you agree with them. It doesn't mean they *are* right. It simply means that you are open to the possibility that they *could* be right. And, sometimes, that's all they're looking for.

Peace. 💭

Every child knows that on Halloween, all they have to do is put on a costume, show up at doors, and say, "Trick or treat" while holding their bag open. In most cases, an adult opens the door and fulfills the request by tossing candy into the bag. The child thanks the adult and skips off to the next house to repeat the process. On occasion, there will be a door with no response. That doesn't stop the child. The child simply leaves that house and goes on to the next in expectation of more candy and corresponding gratitude.

Asking the Universe for what you want is as simple as Trick-or-treating. Know what you want. Ask for it. Be open to receive it. Speak your gratitude. Move gleefully to the next opportunity. It's a sweet deal.

Do you remember dropping your ice cream on the ground as a kid? Or, as a teen, being totally embarrassed in front of your friends? Your first break-up? Your first arrest? Being broke? They all felt like tragedies at the time. As though your life would never be the same. Most likely, you look back at those times now and laugh—or at least see the humor surrounding the situation. You survived and came back smiling.

Tragedy hurts. Loss hurts. Embarrassment hurts. But not forever—unless, of course, you let it. Today's tragedy will be tomorrow's comedy. Sometimes you just have to wait a little while for the laughs.

One thing I hear daily is, "But I keep doing it the same way! How do I change it?"

The answer is simple:

1. Find what you want to change.
2. Find your method of changing it (ie., new thought, new action).
3. PRACTICE. PRACTICE. PRACTICE the new thought or action!

Do you know what "doing it the same way is"? It's PRACTICE! See? You're already a pro at practice! You just have to change what you're practicing.

The way out is the same as the way in.

Years, weeks, days, hours, minutes, seconds. All measures of time that humans made up for their convenience to help describe where we've been, where we are, and where we're going. Yet, in reality, just like air, time just "is." It's ever-present.

We create our own stress when we believe the illusion that time is short and running out. Relax. We are not running out of air. We are not running out of time. Take the pressure off yourself. There is enough time to go around for everyone. Always has been. Always will be.

There's always enough time for you.

One of the deepest self-destructive thoughts we can have, both consciously and unconsciously, is, "I *should be* different." Different—as in: richer, thinner, prettier, younger, smarter, braver, stronger...you get the picture. We beat ourselves up for the things we're not, and it's usually because we want to fit in with somebody else's expectation of who or what we *should* be.

If you have a case of "the shoulds," I invite you to take a look at how many of them are actual "wants." If you *want* to be richer, thinner, prettier, etc., then do it for you! It's much easier to be motivated by a genuine *want* than a fabricated *should*.

Dishonesty can bring on some of the worst-ever feelings and actions. It can destroy trust and faith. It can cause anger, disappointment, doubt, confusion, sadness, and more. Dishonesty can make you lash out, turn your back, or totally withdraw.

Kind of makes you wonder why anyone would choose to be dishonest with themselves, doesn't it?

Honestly.

Does the question "What do I really want?" cause you anxiety? Do you immediately start an inside dialogue that includes, "I don't know what I want—but I should, right? What if I pick the wrong thing? What if I don't deserve it? What will people think if I tell them I want that? What if it's not what *they* want? What if it doesn't work out?"...and on, and on, and on with the voices in your head?

If "What do I really want?" brings you anxiety and keeps you in your head, I invite you to change the question to "What brings me joy?" Joy is a feeling, not a thought. I have a *feeling* that the things that bring you joy will help you determine what you *really* want.

Get out of your head and into your heart.

When it feels like someone else's actions are bringing upheaval or disruption to your life, I invite you to be open to the possibility that, although it may feel catastrophic now, it is most likely opening a door to something better that, without a little push, you might not have ventured out to find.

Trust that it is happening for you, not to you.

In today's social media-speak, FOMO stands for Fear Of Missing Out. So much is constantly happening on Twitter, Facebook, Instagram, etc. and we want to be a part of it. We want to connect, be recognized, have our say, be in-the-know, follow the trends, get the skinny, be like the cool kids. We don't want to miss a thing! It's not just with social media, either. We want to wear the right clothes, frequent the latest restaurants, read the current rag-mags, and be up on today's music. We just want to fit in.

While it feels great to have a connection with others, I invite you to remember to take time to unplug from the social vortex and connect with your *SELF*. Recognize your *SELF*. Get comfortable with your *SELF*. Be amazed by your own being.

Millions of things happen in the world that you aren't a part of. There will be millions more. You can waste time fearing that you're missing out, or you can spend time connecting with yourself and being who you really are. Either way, be assured that the world will keep on turning. It would just seem a shame to find out you missed out on the greatness of YOU.

It's amazing how hard we will work to avoid discomfort. We lie or withhold the truth from ourselves and others, we avoid, overcompensate, give in, withdraw, become martyrs, or overdramatize. We overeat, quit eating, self-medicate and disconnect JUST TO KEEP FROM HURTING.

Ironic, no?

Funny thing is, after feeling all the *added* discomfort caused from avoiding it, the original discomfort will still be there, patiently waiting for us to explore, dissect, and move through it. And when I say patiently, I mean forever...or until we decide to take care of it.

I invite you to explore, dissect, and move through your discomfort rather than using avoidance tactics sooner rather than later. Unless, of course, you like working overtime. 😮

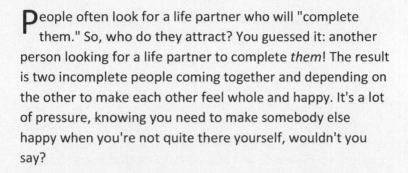

People often look for a life partner who will "complete them." So, who do they attract? You guessed it: another person looking for a life partner to complete *them*! The result is two incomplete people coming together and depending on the other to make each other feel whole and happy. It's a lot of pressure, knowing you need to make somebody else happy when you're not quite there yourself, wouldn't you say?

The foundation of a really grounded relationship is two individual people who are already feeling confident and whole. Then, when they come together, they are a couple who feels even better together. They're free to be who they are because they know their partner is already happy. No pressure. Mission complete.

When you're trying to change an ingrained habit (eating, language, spending, resistance, or reactiveness, for example), success can seem unreachable. You think you have it licked, then *BAM!* There it is again. You're back where you started.

You can think of it that way if you want, or you can see the progress you've made just by being aware that there's still work to be done. Just because you haven't completely changed doesn't mean that you haven't made progress. It just means there's more practice to be done to make the new habits stick. If you really want to make the change, keep practicing. The *BAM!* is part of your awareness, and awareness is progress. ⌐

When you choose to forego a change that you know wholeheartedly is best for you because you're afraid it will hurt you or someone else too much, be prepared to suffer.

How long will you suffer? Until the pain of not changing becomes greater than the fear of making the change.

There is good news, though: you are completely in charge of the length of your suffering. 😮

W e like things easy. Once we find the easy way, we tend
to stick with it until it becomes a habit. Natural. In the
groove. While most of the time creating habits makes our life
run more smoothly, it can also lead us to become
complacent, out of touch with our own bodies, and unaware
of our own thoughts and actions. Robotic, if you will.

I invite you to shake things up. Do something differently
today to bring some awareness into your body and being. It
can be something as simple as brushing your teeth or holding
your coffee cup with your opposite hand. Switch the shoulder
on which you hold your purse. Park in a different spot. Eat at
a different chair at the dinner table. Your brain will say,
"Whoa! That's different!" and your body will make the
needed adjustments. You will bring a new alertness and
awareness to your being.

Small change makes big change.

Forgiveness is not an act of setting somebody else free from pain or guilt or suffering. Do you know why? Because we don't get to choose whether they will choose to be free from pain or guilt or suffering.

Forgiveness is an act of setting *ourselves* free from pain or guilt or suffering. Forgiveness is finding compassion for the reality of the situation and giving ourselves permission to no longer suffer from it. To let go of the painful story. To let go of blame, shame, or guilt. To move forward.

Forgiveness is for *your* freedom from pain, not theirs.

Do you have a story around not being good at creating, using your imagination, or visualizing? (Who do you think is creating that story?) Creating, imagining, and visualizing don't only apply to positive aspects. It could be that you're simply creating, imagining, and visualizing things that give you a more negative vibe. For example, worry is just imagining or visualizing a negative outcome for the future. And, when you start to believe what you are imagining or visualizing to be true, you create that negative outcome. So, the yin and yang of things—the balance of positive and negative—means that positive imagining and visualization will create a positive outcome.

Give it a try. For every situation and challenge you face, I invite you to imagine and visualize the BEST POSSIBLE OUTCOME. Start creating the positive life you want. You have nothing to lose and everything to gain.

Imagine.

Complaining about a recurring dilemma (overspending, overeating, undesirable relationships, unfulfilling jobs, habitual lateness, disconnection from soul, etc.) will not change the dilemma for the better. Complaining is asking the Universe for more of what you don't want.

Focusing more on what you DO want gives the Universe a much clearer set of instructions and sets change for the better into action.

I invite you to be intentional about being complaint-free and focusing more on what you want. Unless, of course, complaining is working for you. 🎯

There is more than one kind of bad planning. There's the "duh" kind, where you simply forget to plan (like forgetting to thaw the turkey before guests start arriving, or making sure your spare tire has air, or building a five-bedroom house with only one bathroom). You may get that head-smack, gut-drop feeling when it happens, but you quickly realize your lack of planning and find a solution.

Then there's the "bad" bad planning, or what we more commonly know as worry. Worry is negative planning in your mind. It is mentally creating and preparing for something you do not want. It is answering all the "what ifs" with a non-pleasing outcome and bracing yourself for pain. Some people worry in order to avoid that head-smack, gut-drop feeling of not planning, while all along not realizing they actually have a steady head-reeling, gut-wrenching feeling from worry. And, worst of all, they don't realize they are creating a vibration that actually summons to them that which they actually do not want.

It seems to me that a quick *smack-in-the-head-and-get-on-with-it* beats summoning negative results—by a landslide. My invitation to you is to plan accordingly!

Researchers have estimated that the average person has between 50,000 and 70,000 thoughts per day.

This is just a reminder that even though they are *your* thoughts, you are not required to believe all of them.

Imagine your life without shame.

Imagine not wishing you were more than you are.

Imagine not feeling the pressure of meeting somebody else's expectations.

Imagine having no worries of imperfection.

Imagine loving yourself through every action or inaction, no matter the outcome.

Imagine accepting your whole self with no hesitation.
Let's all start there and watch the miracles that follow.

If money were falling from the sky, would you rather have a shot glass or a 55-gallon drum to catch it in? I'm guessing your answer would be the 55-gallon drum for the simple reason that the top is more open and the capacity is deeper, making it possible to receive more money.

Yup. Metaphor.

Open your heart and mind to the possibilities. Allow yourself room to receive (and not just money!).

So, you want to change the way you're living? You want a better body? Love life? Job? Attitude? Whatever you want to change, there are many ways to go about it. You can read self-help books, hire a coach, go to therapy, join a 12-step program, get a mentor, attend seminars and retreats, listen to tapes and watch videos, or seek advice from trusted friends. Help is certainly out there. Just remember that all the help in the world won't make a difference if you don't implement it.

You might own a big toolbox of shiny tools, but you're not a carpenter until you use them.

When you meet your truth and decide to make a change in your thinking, feeling, actions, boundaries, and the way you treat yourself, your initial reaction will feel like freedom and/or joy. You'll have an overwhelming feeling of peace and "coming home."

I invite you to embed this feeling in your heart and mind, and make it a practice to remember it often. Why? Because there will be people in your life who will not understand your decision to change or who will disagree with it because it doesn't serve their needs.

They may try to talk you out of changing by degrading you or bullying you or trying to make you feel guilty for wanting what you want. By embedding your feelings of freedom, joy, peace, and coming home, you will strengthen your resolve to make the change for YOU.

The people in your life will either come around to accept your change—or not. That's their decision, not yours.

Come home.

Believe it or not, asking yourself Does it bring me joy? can actually cause stress and anxiety. You may be thinking, "Well, it does make me happy. It does make me feel good. But it's not making me want to dance on the table, so I guess it isn't really bringing me joy."

This kind of confounded thinking comes from believing that joy is always an emotional display of exuberance and exhilaration; that you must be lit with excitement to feel joy. Not true. Joy is the emotion evoked by well-being, success, or good fortune, or by the prospect of possessing what one desires. It's a source or cause of delight. A state of happiness or bliss. Joy has more to do with what you feel on the inside and less to do with how you emote it to the outside world. So, don't sweat It. Nobody gets to define your joy but you.

Tornados touching down create dramatic crises and devastating damage, as do fires, floods, and earthquakes. The landscape instantly and sometimes permanently changes, often leaving scars and evidence of the destruction that seem irreparable. Yet, underneath, with little or no drama, nature immediately starts the healing and reconstruction process. Although the landscape may not take on its original shape, it adopts and breathes new life into its new form, and it carries on. We've come to trust that it will happen because that's what nature does, and we adjust accordingly.

When you experience a dramatic crisis or devastating damage in your life that feels irreparable, remember that you are part of nature. There may be scars and it may take longer than you think it should to repair, but underneath, if you allow it, the healing and reconstruction process will take place. Because when we allow it and trust it, that's what humans do too.

"How am I supposed to know what you're thinking? I'm not a mind reader!" We've all said it at one point or another. Then we probably inwardly (or outwardly) poured on the anger, self-pity, shame, blame or anxiety that the situation rendered. Ugh.

What if we took the drama out of our own words and gave ourselves permission to believe them for what they really are? "How AM I supposed to know what you're thinking? (Ha! Impossible! I cannot control your thoughts, nor is it my job to do so!) I'm NOT a mind reader! I am a _____ (mother, teacher, doctor, attorney, spouse, you get the drift...)" Relieve yourself of the burden of being responsible for what other people think.

Less drama. Just a thought.

The best time to set your intentions for the day, connect with the Universe, and decide to be happy is the exact minute you wake up. But if that doesn't happen, don't stress out. There are 1,439 other best times of the day to do that exact thing. See...timing IS everything!

It's interesting to observe the extent to which we will tolerate our own inner conflict in an effort to avoid what we can only predict or imagine will be outer conflict with another. It's especially interesting to observe how we will blame another for not knowing what we want when it is ourselves who refuse to speak up.

What are you tolerating in yourself that you wouldn't tolerate in others? Who are you blaming for your silence?

What you've been taught and/or programmed to believe is often different from what you truly believe. But what if you're not sure what you truly believe?

Fortunately (yes, fortunately!), when there is a discrepancy between what you've been taught or programmed to believe and what you truly believe, it will show up in your life by means of conflict - inward and/or outward. These conflicts are invitations to question the truth of your beliefs. They present opportunities to change those beliefs that are not serving you or to stand firm in your true beliefs.

When you look at it that way, conflict is just opportunity in disguise.

When you listen with only your ears, you hear what you think is being said and then go into your head to confirm the interpretation. When you also listen with your heart, you feel the deeper and broader message, allowing the opportunity for fuller and better understanding.

Listen and allow.

Procrastination is resistance to your own authority. If you're putting it off, you might want to have a "sit-down" with your boss.

In the Academy Award nominated movie, "Bridge of Spies", an American insurance attorney is recruited to defend an accused Soviet spy in court and then help the CIA facilitate the exchange of the spy for the Soviet-captured American U2 spy plane pilot, Francis Gary Powers. The plot is an intense and emotional chess game as we watch the characters on both sides strategize their next move and agonize over who will do what. The attorney comes to like the Soviet spy, and the respect is mutual. At several intense points in the movie, the attorney asks the spy, "Are you worried?" Each time the spy calmly, innocently, and sincerely turns to the lawyer and responds, "Would it help?"

There is no problem too big or small over which worrying will ever help.

No worries.

When we need it, we tend to think of rest as physical: free of activity, labor, or minimal movement. A good night's sleep or some physical relaxation is a great way to rest. Rest also means peace of mind or spirit, and free from anxieties. Turning off the to-do list, unplugging from electronics, and meditation can give you mental rest.

Whether you have a challenging physical day or a stressful mental day, the rest is up to you.

Rest comfortably. ◎

Just because you don't agree with the beliefs or actions of another (person, company, religion, group), it doesn't mean that everything about them is wrong or bad. To fully reject them because of a partial difference in opinion denies you the opportunity to practice patience, understanding, acceptance, and love and denies them the same. You can set boundaries without building walls. Would you throw the baby out with the bathwater? 💭

One of the greatest benefits of a daily practice of patience is how much easier it makes it to fall into a place of calm when the unexpected arises.

Practice makes patience.

There will be people along your journey who will not grow at the same rate you do. Some won't notice your growth, and some will even deny your growth. They may offer advice and tell you what you should and shouldn't have done or what you should or shouldn't do now or next. I invite you to remember that all of their comments and advice have everything to do with them and where they are or have been. They only know what they know. Bless them for wanting the best for you, and continue to move forward. Only you know what's best for you.

Keep moving.

How do you explain yourself when you're choosing something different than what others want or expect from you? Try these:

This is what I want (or, this isn't what I want)
This feels good to me (or, this doesn't feel good to me)
I'm choosing something different

That's it. No need to elaborate or trail off into a lengthy apologetic excuse or justification of your choice to fit their needs. This is your choice.

Plain. Simple. Powerful.

It's crazy how much easier it is for people to hear and understand what you want them to hear and understand when you actually say the words out loud. In other words, they can't listen if you're not actually talking.

Say it with love.

If you're wanting to:
          set some boundaries for yourself
            steer clear of overwhelm
                 practice staying in your own business
        let go of the need to control
           reduce worry

here are a few helpful mantras to repeat:

      "Not mine to fix."
          "Not mine to solve."
              "No obligation to volunteer."
      "Not my duty to make it right."
         "Not my circus. Not my monkeys."

Rinse. Repeat. Relax.

Even if you see the glass as half empty, you still have the option of drinking what's left and refilling. Options abound when you're looking for them.

You know those things you bemoan and put off? Things like working out, cleaning your desk, changing your eating habits, doing your taxes, or tackling a big project.

The tasks that feel so overwhelming to start that you find every excuse not to start, even though you know that when you've finished, you'll feel so happy?

One of the reasons we don't start is that we've already planted the thought in our head that it's going to be hard or boring or time consuming. We are focused on the potentially bad part of the experience. When faced with this challenge, I invite you to immediately focus on the good part and visually create your success in your mind. Imagine yourself getting off the treadmill, sitting behind your clean desk, admiring your healthy body, mailing that envelope, or celebrating the successful completion of your project. Hold that vision in your mind and that feeling in your body. Now ask yourself, "What is the first thing I need to do to get to that fabulous place?" and do it.

If that doesn't work, ask yourself this: "Do I want to feel good about myself today, or would I rather beat myself up and feel bad?" ALWAYS YOUR CHOICE.

On your mark, get set...

Y ou can't give someone something you don't have. To be of ultimate service on this planet, fill yourself up first and then be totally generous with the overflow.

Love me some leftovers!

D id your intentions for the day include wasting time on social media or a phone app? Did they include avoiding your feelings? Did they include fog-eating, lethargy, or worrying about money? Did you write your intentions down so you could check in with them during your day?

You did set your intentions, right?

Many say, "I want security" or "I want to feel secure." What they really want is a guarantee that they will not feel pain.

Webster defines security as safety, freedom from worry, and protection." If you yearn for security, it could be that you're in a constant state of doubt, a feeling of lack, expecting the bad in everything, and/or not trusting that the Universe is working in your favor. Sound familiar?

Security from outside sources is an illusion. There are no guarantees that you will not feel pain at least once (or many times) in your life. Pain is part of the process of being human. It's part of the process of growth. The feeling of security is totally an inside job, and the more you set your sights on simply being happy, the more secure you will feel.

Overwhelm isn't caused by having too much to do. Overwhelm is caused by not honoring your own boundaries and by forgetting that nobody can do it all, nobody is supposed to do it all, and it will never all be done.

You do have boundaries, don't you?

Holding a grudge does not protect you from being hurt in the future. It only keeps you living in your unwanted past.

If you are holding a grudge, I invite you to acknowledge the reality that whatever happened happened, and it's over now. You can choose to change present and future interactions with this person by setting firm boundaries, but there is no room for the other person to change or make amends with you if you insist on only seeing them as they were in your unwanted past.

Move on. 🚩

Our eyes can only see the surface. Everything underneath the surface is only perceived. It is only what we believe is there or should be there—until we go deeper and the truth is revealed.

I invite you to take the time to go deeper. Sometimes, something better to believe is hiding just below the surface.

That's deep. 🎯

The worldwide odds of being a victim of shark attack are 1 in 2,535,633,900.

The nationwide (US) odds of being a victim of a lightning strike are 1 in 700,000.

The universal odds of you allowing yourself to be a victim of your own negativity, limiting thoughts and fears, is a chance over which you get 100% control.

What are the odds that you'll choose to be a victim unto yourself today? I invite you to shoot for 0%. 😮

Here's a crazy question: What are you pretending not to know?

>"I don't know what I want."
>"I don't know how to get what I want."
>"I don't know what to do next."

Ring any bells?

Here's another crazy question for you: What are you avoiding by pretending not to know?

>"Having to take responsibility."
>"Having to take action."
>"Stepping up into who I really am."

Ring any bells?

Guess what. You can own that you really DO know——and you still choose to avoid it. Honesty is empowering. And here's a little secret...if you own what you know, you may find less reason to avoid it.

It's an amazing feeling when, after years and years of holding yourself back, you find the deep, limiting belief that's been causing all your pain. Eureka! You're cured! Now your life will change immediately! And then it doesn't, and you don't know why.

Finding the limiting belief is only one part of the healing and growing process.

Replacing the limiting belief with a new, truer thought and belief is the next important part. Practicing the new, truer thought and belief until it is second-nature and automatic is the most important (and most rigorous and time-intensive) part of the process. Remember, you practiced that limiting belief for years! Your thoughts need a new path to travel. Practicing the new thought and belief will beat that new path into existence.

Practice. Practice. Practice. 🎯

Throughout the course of history and in every generation, there has been illness, disappointment, disaster, hate, tragedy, famine, deceit, war, poverty, destruction, and death. There has also been healing, satisfaction, growth, love, beauty, abundance, truth, peace, community, fulfillment, birth, and even rebirth.

Through all of this, the world, in all its wisdom, continues to turn. And every moment of every day you get to choose between: "Will I focus on the good, or will I focus on the bad?" Either way, the world will continue to turn, giving you, every single day, a new opportunity to choose.

Every. Single. Day.

There will always be more to do, more to read, more to learn, more to give, more to see, more to achieve, more, more, more. Always.

It's up to you to determine what is enough for today.

Enough said.

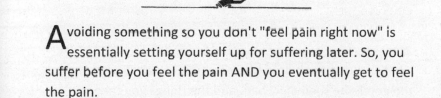

To proclaim that you will "live fearlessly (without fear) from this point forward" is exhilarating and impressive. Good luck with that!

You may find it easier, however, to simply live intentionally and consciously with less fear and more self-confidence.

To fear less is a totally achievable goal. 😯

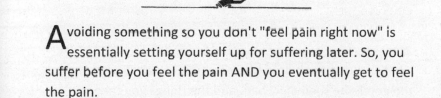

Avoiding something so you don't "feel pain right now" is essentially setting yourself up for suffering later. So, you suffer before you feel the pain AND you eventually get to feel the pain.

If it's happiness you're shopping for, I invite you to ask yourself, "Is that 2-for-1 really a bargain?" Choosing to suffer seems more like paying double the price.

Shop wisely, my friend.

The amount of time you spend wearily treading water in survival mode depends on how long it takes you to remember that you can swim. Most likely, if you simply stretch a little and stand up, you'll discover that the water isn't as deep as you believe it is.

Short and sweet: Gratitude is the quickest way to feel abundance, breathe happiness, and step into a place of empowerment.

Whatever your mood or situation today, I invite you to take periodic breaks and drop into gratitude for all that you have: the good, the seemingly bad, and the things you take for granted such as the blue sky, clean drinking water, and Cocoa Krispies. Quickly name five things you're grateful for each time you take a break and observe your happiness meter. I bet it rises.

Short and sweet. That's how we roll.

The sea captain of a cargo ship sets a schedule and charts a course to the port where he will deliver his cargo. On schedule, he pulls anchor and gets underway. The water is smooth for the first few days, but then an unexpected storm appears. The ship is tossed and pitched and blown off course. When the storm subsides, the captain has two choices. He can either right and repair his ship, allowing him to get back on course, or he can give up and sit adrift in the middle of the ocean, going nowhere and delivering nothing.

When an intention or plan you've set meets with unexpected circumstances, you can choose to get back on course or to give up.

Experience tells us that moving forward feels better than drifting aimlessly. I invite you to remember that you are always the captain of your ship. 🎯

Sometimes the reason we give up on our dreams is that we only create the glorious successful outcome in our imagination, and we forget the "journey" part that comes along with it. Then, when we hit a bump in the road or meet with a challenge—or what we might call a "failure"—we conclude that our dream is unreachable.

What's more likely is that your dream is totally reachable, but you expected it to be much easier to reach.

I invite you to dream and dream BIG! And while you're dreaming, imagine yourself brilliantly solving challenges, diligently forging obstacles, and courageously overcoming failures along the way. That way, you won't be blindsided by them and the entire journey will feel successful.

Dream really BIG! 🔵

The first step to getting somewhere is deciding that you're not going to stay where you are. Once you really decide and commit, the way will show itself. 🎯

You can armor yourself with ammunition to win an argument for ego's sake, or you can open yourself up to gain more understanding for love's sake.

Which feels more like the real win?

Imagine being in a terrible drought, knowing that rain will eventually come but not knowing when. Would you sit inside with the lids tight on your buckets, anxiously trying to predict when the rain will arrive so you can open your buckets and run them outside to catch it? Or, would you remain ever-ready by opening the lids and setting the buckets outside, confident that they will catch the rain whenever it decides to fall while you patiently go about your business?

Knowing what you want is only one part of manifesting. Alignment, faith, and being open to receive in Divine timing are the other parts.

I invite you to pop some lids! Keep your buckets open and outside today and every day to catch all that the Universe has to offer in its Divine timing.

Your resistance to the answer doesn't mean that the answer is wrong.

Are you willing to do what it takes to get what you really want? Answer these questions:

What am I willing to try?
What/who am I willing to let go of?
What action am I willing to take?
What beliefs am I willing to change?
What changes am I willing to embrace?
How much time/energy am I willing to spend?
How much discomfort am I willing to endure?
How much fear am I willing to explore?

And now for the big question: how long am I willing to sit around and hope it will happen by itself?

Are you willing? Let's get this party started.

Often the "worst thing that could happen" is that you choose to spend your time frozen in fear worrying about "the worst thing that could happen."

When was the last time you apologized for breathing? Do you feel shame every time you stand up, sit down, or take a step? Do you worry that your constant heartbeat is offending others? Do you have guilt around your circulatory system? My guess is, your answers are: never, no, no, and no. Of course not! These are all part of being human! We don't think twice about how our body is functioning. We didn't have to learn how to make it work. It just comes naturally.

Why, then, do we feel such shame and guilt around emotions? Why do we apologize for showing or expressing our feelings? Why do we apologize for crying or being angry or confused? The answer is, it's what we've been taught to do to make others comfortable. That's what we've learned.

Emotions are part of the human experience. They are natural. They are necessary. They are vital to living a full and enriched life. I invite you to be open to unlearning to feel shame around showing emotion. There is no need to apologize for being human.

Have you ever been out to dinner with a friend who invariable asks to modify the menu?

"Could you please leave out the onion and instead replace it with a little sautéed minced garlic—not pressed, minced—and instead of the potatoes, I'd like a side salad with grated parmesan instead of cheddar. And, can I get a glass of room-temperature water with a rosemary sprig instead of lemon?"

The waitstaff may roll their eyes, but they place the order, and most times, the modified menu item appears for your friend.

If you also tend to roll your eyes at your friend and wonder why she can't just order off the menu like everyone else, I invite you to notice that your friend is courageous and confident enough to ask for what she wants. Instead of rolling your eyes, I invite you to lift your eyebrows and take the opportunity to ask for what you want. Sure, there's a small chance you might not get it, but what is the risk of asking?

You know we're not just talking about modifying menus here, right? ⚡

No matter how much it appears that some things never change, one thing will always be true: you can always change your thoughts around them.

Not always easy, but always true.

Always.

Three good reasons to visit your past:
- To savor and vibrate in happy memories and successes
- To remind yourself of valuable lessons and experiences you've had
- To reflect on how far you've come in your journey

Three less-than-good and most likely damaging reasons to visit your past:
- To renew your painful story (allowing you to stay in it for a variety of reasons, including sympathy, attention seeking, and martyrdom)
- To beat yourself up and validate your feelings of being "not enough"
- To avoid obvious and scary changes that lie in front of you

If it's still not clear, the first three reasons are probably your best choice. But then again, it IS your choice.

When we talk about taking things personally, we normally think about how we're affected by someone else's words and actions. Do you think you're pretty solid when it comes to not taking things personally? "Sticks and stones can break your bones" and all that stuff, right?

What about when your boss tells you what a great job you did? Or when your child or partner hugs you and says, "I love you so much"? Don't you take those things personally? How about when you look in the mirror and beat yourself up? That's the ultimate example of taking it personally.

Just to be clear, we take everything personally. We take comments and bits of information "into our person." It's from there that we process what we are making it mean and how we feel about it. It's from there that we can explore whether or not it's true for us. It allows us to practice and grow and learn.

I invite you to go ahead and take things personally. Just remember to complete the process of asking yourself, "What am I making it mean?" and find out if it's really true.

The frustration and worry you feel regarding what others do or don't do is really all about your own potential unease. For example, you may find yourself thinking, "If they do/don't do _____, I will feel sad, lonely, angry, overwhelmed, pained, embarrassed, unloved, overworked, financially burdened, stressed for time, trapped, afraid, lost, etc." No matter what they do, you are consciously or unconsciously predicting how their actions will negatively affect you.

You may be saying, "But I'm worried they won't be happy or successful." That's still about you! If they are not happy or successful, it affects you in no way, unless you decide that it does.

It's great to care about the well-being of others. It's great to hope and wish for others' happiness and success. I invite you to remember, however, that we each have our own path and responsibility for our own happiness.

Perhaps your energy would be better spent predicting how your own positive actions will affect you and your potential ease, since that's really all you can control.

There's a big difference between "I feel" and "I am."

While there are several reasons you might choose to feel angry, frustrated, depressed, sad, bored, confused, depleted, overwhelmed, unsatisfied, or not enough, there are very few reasons, if any, why you would choose to BE any of those things.

I invite you to be aware of the language you use when describing your negative emotions. Instead of saying out loud or to yourself, "I AM depressed, angry, sad, etc...," practice saying, "I FEEL depressed, angry, sad, etc...". You may notice that the word FEEL helps keep the burden on the outside edges, further from your heart. 🔵

Your message may not be received as you intended even when you center yourself, come from a place of truth and peace, choose your words with love and kindness, and deliver your message as clearly and succinctly as possible. That's because you never get to choose how someone else receives it or what they make it mean. It can be so frustrating, can't it?

I invite you to deliver the message anyway, remembering that:

- they may not be as open to change as you are
- it may not be their truth
- they may be suffering from something you are unaware of
- they are on their own path, not yours
- all timing is Divine

Whether they receive it in the manner you intend or not, you'll have peace of mind and heart knowing you are operating within your own truth and integrity. 🎯

In a jam? Stuck on a decision? Can't figure out why you keep repeating the same behavior? Maybe you're forgetting to play the warmer/colder game. Here's a review of how to play:

1. Figure out or remember WHAT YOU REALLY WANT (REALLY IMPORTANT STEP!).
2. Ask yourself, "If I do this (don't do this/think this/say this/don't say this...), will it take me closer (warmer) or further away (colder) from WHAT I REALLY WANT?"
3. Proceed toward the things that feel warmer.
4. Steer away from the things that feel colder.

NOTE: This game has no ending and allows for endless do-overs, if needed.

That thing that's been bugging the heck out of you...

What if it weren't a problem today?
What if it simply didn't matter—just for today?
What if you didn't give it another ounce of attention?

Just for today.

Breathe in that feeling. Now exhale.

Picture in your mind a trapeze artist, floating through the air from bar to bar until she reaches the next platform. Beautiful. Graceful. Confident. How does she make her daring journey look so easy? If you asked her, she would probably reply: "All you have to do to move forward is let go of the last bar."

Yes, metaphor.

What are you holding on to? Jump, release, and float with the greatest of ease.

Universe: Knock. Knock.
  Us: Who's there?
Universe: Love. Joy. Compassion. Peace. Freedom. Fun.
Everything you ever wanted.
Us: Please! Come in! We've been waiting our whole lives for you!
Universe: You have to open your door first.

When opportunity knocks, don't forget to open the door.

The biggest business challenge we face every day is simply staying in our own business.

- not attaching to other people's judgments
- not judging others
- not trying to fix or control others
- being compassionate with ourselves
- allowing things to be what they are

Are you up for this business challenge today? The returns are astounding.

Listening with an open mind means you clear your thoughts of preconceived opinions, beliefs, or past-given meanings to consider that which you are receiving. It means you are open to all possibilities and willing to let go of expectation. It means you are giving yourself the gift of freedom to choose how you feel in that present moment instead of automatically relying on learned responses, reactions, emotions, or stories from the past. It is a willingness to look beyond the confines of your own walls.

I invite you to knock down some walls. Listen with an open mind today and discover the freedom to choose from infinite possibilities.

Which is better: doing the hard stuff first and getting it out of the way, or doing the easy stuff first and inching into the hard stuff? There is no definitive answer; it all depends on you. But either choice is better than living in an indecisive limbo state.

What do you really want? Fast or slow, big or small, hard or easy—I invite you to keep your eyes on the prize and just make a move in that direction.

Y ou can let go of the belief that everything that's happening right now should make sense, then simply hold faith that the Universe is working in your best and highest good in Divine timing,

or

You can hold tight to that belief and keep struggling to make absolute sense of things in hope that controlling it will guarantee your eventual happiness.

Hmmmm. Tough choice. In the end, it will all work out. Why make it harder than it has to be?

Sometimes what we label our own trust issues are simply memories of past hurts or traumas we've yet to resolve or haven't released. They are trying to protect us from being hurt again.

Sometimes our trust issues are actually our intuition at work, informing us that something is not as it appears, is out of integrity, or is "rotten in Denmark."

If we have the first kind of trust issue, it often leads to the heightening of our intuition. If we follow our intuition, we often get to avoid the first kind of trust issue.

Either way, I invite you to trust that it all works out when you allow it to.

Some people spend their whole lives trying to prove to everyone else that they are good enough without ever stopping to consider, "What is good enough for me?"

There's no need to prove to anyone else that you are good enough. You already are. You always will be. You came here that way. I invite you to let go of measuring your value and worth with somebody else's yardstick. Why fight for the hope of receiving their inches when you can more blissfully give yourself miles?

Conflict doesn't come from people having different beliefs. Conflict comes from thinking others should believe the same way you do.

As long as there are different beliefs, there will always be choices when it comes to what to believe. You have the freedom to choose to change or to never change your beliefs. I invite you to allow others the same freedom.

Conflicts averted.

Rushing ahead and living in the future where nothing is happening right now leaves a big hole in your present, where everything is happening right now.

Hmmmm. Feels like "right now" is the place to be.

The underlying thought in almost every drama is "This is not what I want." From that thought, you can either choose to resist and fight in an attempt to get what you want (fear-driven action), or you can align yourself with what you want and allow space for it to come (love-driven action).

Fear feeds drama. Alignment diffuses it. What do you really want? How will you choose to get it?

Aligning is the better answer.

Some of the best gifts you'll ever receive, some of the greatest experiences you'll ever have, and some the best feelings you'll ever feel often happen when you throw your hands in the air and sincerely release your desire to control the outcome.

Let it be. It is what it is. "Whatever happens, happens. I give up."

Relax and wait for the beautiful results.

It's amazing how making the smallest changes can create big shifts when you're longing for something that seems impossible to achieve.

Longing for more rest? Try going to bed two minutes earlier for a week.
Longing for more time? Try getting up two minutes earlier for a week.
Longing for a healthier body? Try drinking one extra glass of water per day.
Longing for more money? Try setting aside one dollar a day for a week.

This may sound too simple and too small to make a difference. However, if you will take the time and effort to make small changes, you will find that what you are creating is a shift in your awareness, in the ways you think and act. Small changes are easily practiced. Small changes build confidence. Small changes open bigger doors.

Never underestimate the power of small change.

What if instead of saying "I'll be so happy when this is done," you make the decision to also be happy while you're doing it?

Two birds. One stone.

Double your pleasure!

No matter how well or for how long you've known someone,
you still can only predict how they will feel or react.

Or, you can have an expectation of how they should feel or react.

When it's all said and done, you have no control over how they feel or react.

We often think of taking a leap of faith as being very scary and overwhelming. The phrase "leap of faith" means "an act of believing in or attempting something whose existence or outcome cannot be proved." That's it. That's all it is. Though you may not realize it, you are taking leaps of faith daily:

- You get in your car to go to work. You can't see your workplace, but you believe it will be there where you get there.
- You put your clothes in the washer, turn it on, and walk away believing that the cycle will finish, and your clothes will be cleaned.
- You kiss your spouse or kids goodbye and wish them a nice day, believing you will see them when they get home.
- You buy a watermelon, believing it will taste as good on the inside as it looks and sounds on the outside.

These and so many, many other things we do each day are actually just little leaps of faith. A part of life. The way we move.

If you are holding yourself back from something because it requires a scary leap of faith on your part, I invite you to look at all the evidence that you are already a pro at leaping. Remember, you can be afraid AND believe at the same time.

We are all living day-to-day, leap-by-leap. That's it. That's all it is. 😲

If you feel depressed or angry from watching the news or reading the paper, remember, you can choose not to.

If you dread answering the phone or meeting up with someone who's company you don't enjoy, remember, you can choose not to.

If you detest going to obligatory functions, shopping malls, or your in-laws' house, remember, you can choose not to. You can even choose to not go to work, to school, or to the doctor.

Choices are made based on your level of comfort and courage around its consequences or perceived consequences. You are never without choice.

When you're contemplating your choices, I invite you to consider this question: Am I willing to feel a little uncomfortable in the moment in order to feel a lot happier in the long run?

The choice is yours.

When you were young, you probably believed the story of the tooth fairy that's been passed down from generation to generation. When you discovered there was no tooth fairy, you were most likely disappointed, but you accepted that it was just a "story" and simply dropped your previous belief.

There were most likely many other "stories" you learned that you turned into beliefs. Some may have been passed down from generation to generation, either consciously or unconsciously. Some may have been about your limited self-worth or apparent shortcomings, and you're still believing them today. I invite you to explore those stories. What if, like the tooth fairy, you discovered that these stories not only aren't true today but they never were?

What if you accepted that they were just stories and simply dropped your beliefs?

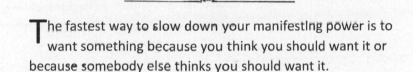

Instead of being against hate, be for love.
    Instead of being against violence, be for peace.
        Instead of being against prejudice, be for equality.
    Instead of being against control, be for freedom.
        Instead of being against mediocrity, be for greatness.
    Instead of opposing, be inclusive. 🎯

The fastest way to slow down your manifesting power is to want something because you think you should want it or because somebody else thinks you should want it.

You can still manifest it the slow way, but don't you have better things to want with your time? 💭

N eed some ideas for setting intentions? Here are several.

"It is my intention...":

to operate from a place of peace and centeredness
to speak the language of love more than fear
to honor my inner wisdom and my body
to let go of the things I cannot control
to be easy with myself and others
to find the humor in daily living

Get the idea? When you live with intention, you create your own happiness.

Y ou don't need anybody else's permission to be happy or make changes in your own life. It is helpful, however, for you to give yourself permission for these things to happen.

If you're feeling frustrated, angry, confused, scared, lonely or lost, remember that sometimes, you need to lose your balance in order to create a more solid foundation on which to build your amazing new life.

In other words, even the seemingly bad is good.

The great thing about the truth is that it's always kInd enough to wait around until you're ready to accept it. It totally lets you decide how long you're willing to suffer beforehand.

Interestingly enough, the root of feeling overwhelmed as well as its opposite, feeling bored, seems to stem from one common denominator: not taking time to care for one's own personal happiness, well-being, and peace.

You first; what a concept.

You cannot be fully open to receiving that which is in your best and highest good if you are not willing to let go of that which is not serving you.

What can you let go of today? The Universe is looking for clear space to fill up your basket.

They say you shouldn't take that risk.
    They say you should be working harder.
        They say you don't need those things you
        really want.
They say you need to be more like everyone else.
    They say you should be afraid, happier, smarter.
        They say blah, blah, blah, blah, blah.

Who are they? And moreover, how do they know what you
need, want, should, or shouldn't do or have?

We all have these people in our lives. While they may mean
well, keep in mind that they are basing their comments on
their own beliefs and experiences. They are not YOU. They do
not know YOUR heart or YOUR path.

I invite you to thank them for their advice and
recommendations, and for giving you the opportunity to
choose to follow your own heart, mind, and path. Then tune
in to YOU. Who knows...they may be amazed by your
choices!

God/The Universe never punishes us and never needs to. We do a good enough job of that ourselves. 💭

The human eye is able to distinguish over 10 million different colors. Ten million! Why is it, then, that we expect and sometimes literally force our brains and thoughts to see and process things as only black or white?

I invite you to open your eyes, your mind, and your heart to all the colors of what's happening around you and for you and consider how others may be seeing things differently. The Universe is offering over 10 million different colors. Perhaps it's time to step away from the confines of black and white. 📚

To be fearless is to be in total lack of fear. We're often prompted to be fearless in the pursuit of our dreams, yet in reality, most humans experience some kind of fear every day. There may be many things you do that feel less scary, but if you worry, you have fear. If you avoid, you have fear. If you're stuck, you have fear.

What if, instead of striving to be fearless (which often brings more fear in the form of anxiety), we move toward feeling "fearlesser?" Acknowledge your fear, but give it less attention and less power. Talk to fear and say, "I see you, fear. I know you're there. Today, I'm choosing to move forward despite your presence."

Instead of fighting to be fearless today, I invite you to move toward fearing lesser than you did yesterday. As you move more fear-lesser-ly, you'll most likely find that the things you fear are not as powerful as you once thought they were. 😮

Some people think enlightenment comes from asking yourself the tough "Why do I...?" "What should I...?" "How do I...?" "When should I...?" "Where will I...?" questions.

Not true. Enlightenment comes from actually answering them.

When you feel frustrated or angry over a recent kerfuffle or argument, and you want to quickly return to center, try this:

Stop any motion (including driving), close your eyes, and un-clench your teeth.

Slow your breathing and repeat this phrase five times on your deep inhale: "It will get better," then blowing out on your exhale.

Slow your breathing even more and repeat this phrase five times on your deep inhale: "It's getting better," then gently blowing out on your exhale.

Breathe deeply and naturally and repeat this phrase five times on your inhale: "It's already better," gently releasing your exhale.

Though whatever led you to feel frustrated or angry may still be happening, you now have changed your energy and can choose to approach the solution from a more centered place.

One way to make things easier is to first believe that it can be easier. Then, from there, allow it to be easier.

If you find yourself in a constant loop, asking the question, "Why does this keep happening to me?", it's most likely because you're not digging deep enough to discover the real answer due to fear. If you seriously want to make a change, give yourself permission to be brave enough to face your truth. Scary? Maybe. But it beats going in circles.

There is no "one size fits all" when it comes to right and wrong or good and bad. We each wear them differently; some more tightly and some more loosely.

Instead of jumping on the latest trend of right and wrong or good and bad and judging others for their choices, I invite you to choose what's comfortable for you and then wear it well. Your truth will never go out of style.

Nobody wants to stub their toe and feel the excruciating pain that comes from it, but the fear of that pain doesn't keep us from walking every day. For most of us, the fear of stubbing our toe doesn't enter our minds on a daily basis. When (or if) it happens, we hop around, maybe curse, feel the pain until it subsides, and then get up and start walking again. We don't dredge up the pain of all of our stubbed toes from the past.

It's funny how fear of emotional pain, even when it isn't currently happening, can keep us paralyzed. We will go so far as to reach back in our history to feel the pain again and again and tell ourselves we can't move forward because it might happen, it will hurt again.

I invite you to remember that the pain of the past is not happening now. Unless you derive great pleasure from pain, it doesn't serve you to keep reliving it. Hop around and curse if you must, then get up and start walking again. 😲

When you've been yearning for change but not taking steps toward it, the Universe provides you with an unexpected catalyst. It's often uncomfortable—mentally, emotionally, and physically. It may feel like you're taking steps backward from any progress you've made. And it's often exactly what you need to nudge you enough to move forward and make the change you're yearning for.

Embrace the catalyst. The change you're yearning for is on the way. 📚

So, you're ready to bust a new move but thoughts appear in your brain, such as:

"There are rules about that." "You shouldn't do that." "That's not the way it's done." "Good girls/boys don't act that way."

"Who do you think you are?" "Who gave you permission to...?" "They're not going to like you if you..." and these thoughts are keeping you from doing what you long to do.

I invite you to ask yourself, "Who's rulebook am I following? Is it working for me?" Maybe it's time to write your own. ⬤

Faith isn't always a leap. Sometimes it's just one little step after another, with lots of falling down and getting back up in between.

Printed on a coffee mug. Seriously.

GPS offers amazing guidance asking only two questions: Where are you now? and Where do you want to go? It then charts the best course for you to reach your final destination. Sometimes it guides you via the shortest distance. Sometimes it guides you via the least amount of time. You pick a route, trust it, and take off in the direction it tells you to go.

Here's what GPS doesn't ask you: Where have you been? How long were you there? Why did you stay so long? What are you afraid of?

It also does not suggest that you travel halfway to your destination and then turn around and go back because it doesn't believe you'll make it.

Where are you now? Where do you want to go? Tune in to your inner GPS. It knows how to get you there if you follow its directions.

Although it is said that "nothing is impossible," I offer you this list of things that are highly improbable should you choose to attempt them:

> making others happy (always their choice)
>> making others obey or concede to power (always their choice)
>>> making others like you (always their choice)
> making others care or not care (always their choice)
>> making others feel guilty (always their choice)

Rather than try to achieve the impossible through others, I invite you to place your energy into choosing to make yourself happy and remembering that "they" all have their hands full doing the same for themselves.

It's true that technology changes lives. It also tends to change expectations of ourselves and others and makes us forget we are still human. We still require time to process thoughts as do others. Just because we have the capability to answer or respond in the blink of an eye does not mean we are obligated to do so.

I invite you to take the time to align with your thoughts and emotions before hurrying to meet the perceived expectations of others, especially through technology. Know your truth. Communicate your truth in your time. The truth is always worth the wait.

One of the bravest things you'll ever have to do in order to move forward is let go of your attachment to the past.

Be brave. Your magnificent future depends on it. 🎯

Sometimes we are so laser-focused on trying to fix what is wrong in our lives that it fills our field of vision and we miss the bigger peripheral picture, which includes all the things that are going right in our lives. If this is happening for you, I invite you to soften your focus. Step back and look at your life as a whole. Look at all the great things that are also happening right before your eyes. Gather evidence for the good. And give thanks.

They say you shouldn't judge people. However, judging is what we humans do. We judge what feels good or not so good. We judge what we like and don't like. We judge what looks or feels different from what we're used to. We judge others in comparison to ourselves and our beliefs. Humans should judge because they do judge. It's how we make our way.

Perhaps "they" are confusing judgment with criticism.

How do you feel about yourself? What's your opinion about the subject? What do you believe are your greatest assets? What do you love about yourself? What do you see in yourself that others may be misinterpreting? What do you know about yourself to be true?

You will never know your true self-worth if you keep comparing yourself to others or let others' opinions of you be variables in your own determination.

Self-worth. It's all about YOU. YOU. YOU. Be for yourself. You're worth it!

You're not running out of time. You may miss an opportunity. You may not meet a deadline or an expectation. You may have another birthday sooner than seems possible. But you are not running out of time. Time is always there for you. Time is at least one step ahead of you.

I invite you to make better friends with time. It never fails to greet you each morning.

It never fails to pave the way for new opportunities, new deadlines, new expectations, and even more birthdays.

Do you find yourself commonly using the word never? As in:

- I'll never find another partner, job, pair of shoes...like I had before
- I'll never be a writer, a good parent, rich, thin
- I'll never have true love, money, freedom
- I'll never take a risk, put myself out there, allow myself to be vulnerable

Never is a shut-off switch. Your vibration tells the Universe what you want. When you vibrate the negative never thoughts and beliefs, you're shutting off opportunities and blessings the Universe wants to give to you. You are telling it, "No, thank you. I'd rather not have that."

Ready to turn that never around? Try this instead:

- I'm open to receiving another great partner, job, shoes
- I'm open to being a writer, a good parent, rich, thin
- I'm open to feeling true love, financial abundance, freedom
- I'm open to trying new things, having new experiences, allowing myself to feel

Then say, "This, or something better, in my highest good and your Divine timing" and allow it to happen. You control the switch.

When you're standing at the threshold of making an exciting, life-changing decision, fearful naysayers will often utter, "Once you step through that door, there's no going back."

I offer you this potential response: "Why would I want to go back?"

We tend to spend a tremendous amount of time doing everything we can to save us from the possibility of being hurt emotionally. We avoid, lie, deny, cheat, blame, shame, pretend, withdraw, cover-up, shut-down, and self-medicate in an effort to "not feel bad." Wow. We feel bad so we don't feel bad. What a concept.

If only there were a way to stop and actually feel your emotions all the way through with curiosity, compassion, and understanding so you would no longer waste time fearing them.

Hey! Wait a minute...

Just feel it.

Waiting is part of the process of manifesting. You can fill your waiting time with negative thoughts about how it isn't coming or the idea that it's taking too long (which, of course, makes the wait longer), or you can trust that it's coming and fill your waiting time doing things that make you happy and thinking positive thoughts about receiving what you asked for, which tends to speed up the process.

Either way, the timing will be what it will be, and it will be perfect. You just get to decide in which mood you want to spend it.

Where are you holding back?
What truth are you avoiding?
Why?
How is that working for you?
When will you change it?

It's your own greatness that's asking, not me.

It's hot outside. / It's too hot outside!

That meal was expensive. / That meal was too expensive!
The music is loud. / The music is too loud!
My pants are tight. / My pants are too tight!
I am afraid. / I am too afraid!

Funny how one little word can change a simple fact into a dramatic complaint. Which feels better, smoother, calmer, easier?

Don't make it too dramatic.

Is there something you do or believe that doesn't feel quite right or that you question the necessity of or the reason for, yet you keep doing it or believing it anyway because that's what you were taught?

You're all grown up now. It's okay to think or do differently. It's okay to feel good and honest about what you do and what you believe. It's okay to question and explore.

I invite you to give yourself permission to be open to the possibility that things can be different from what you were taught.

We tend to use the word "hard" a lot. Life is hard. Relationships are hard. Work is hard. Raising kids is hard. Exercise is hard. Making money is hard. Losing weight is hard. Growing is hard. Putting ourselves out there is hard. Losing someone is hard. Sticking with it is hard. Staying positive is hard. While it's true that these things may require a great deal of endurance or effort, you may be using the word "hard" as a disguise to avoid a different feeling. Instead of taking that shortcut, I invite you to ask yourself:

Is it hard? Or is it uncomfortable?
Is it hard? Or is it undesirable?
Is it hard? Or is it unpleasant?
Is it hard? Or is it unfamiliar?
Is it hard? Or is it different?
Is it hard? Or is it tedious?
Is it hard? Or is it boring?
Is it hard? Or is it scary?

The more honest you are with yourself about your feelings, the easier and more clear your life becomes. In the end, you may find it's really not that hard at all. ⌕

You can be an off-the-charts genius and use logic to solve some of the world's most challenging problems, but you can't think your way to a solution when your challenge involves matters of your heart.

If you are faced with a personal challenge that you can't seem to solve or fix, I invite you to give your brain permission to shut off logic for a while and connect with your feelings. Explore how you're currently feeling and why, then ask yourself how you want to feel. Let your heart talk and listen to it.

As smart as we all think we are, there's still a lot to learn when we listen to our hearts.

Everyone leaves a legacy, which is "anything handed down from the past, as from an ancestor or predecessor." That means that everyone comes into this world receiving automatic influence from others' legacies.

I invite you to remember that just because you were influenced by somebody else's legacy, you can choose not to hand it down if it doesn't serve you. You are creating your own legacy by the way you live and the choices you make each day. What kind of legacy do you want to leave? ⚑

Look at your day. What do you have planned and why? I invite you to savor the experience with the "why" in mind. If you're with family or friends because you're looking for connection and love, savor it when you get it. If you're working on a project or doing chores because you want to accomplish something, savor the accomplishment.

Sometimes we just move through our day, plan in hand, checking things off the list. Today, remember your why. Savor the feelings. Celebrate. Be grateful. It is what you intended, remember? 🎯

Being right and enlightenment are not one in the same. In fact, enlightenment often evolves from your acceptance of not being right.

It is said, "It's better to be alone than to be with someone that makes you feel alone." One more very good reason to know and really love yourself.

Have you ever kept repeating an activity or behavior that you want to change but you just don't seem to have the willpower to make it happen?

- You want to lose weight, but you keep eating junk.
- You want to exercise, but you make excuses for why you can't go to the gym or get out of bed.
- You want to save money, but you keep using your charge card for convenience or impulse purchases.
- You want to end a bad relationship, but you keep tolerating the pain.

That's because willpower feels like restraint and control. It feels like forcing yourself to do something you don't want to do. It's like, "I want it, but I know it's going to feel bad," and who wants to feel bad?

Instead of beating yourself up or making excuses for having little or no willpower, I invite you to focus on boosting your want-power. Ask yourself: how do I want my body, my finances, my relationships to feel? Why do I want it? When do I want it? What's it going to take from me to get what I want? The more positively you visualize and focus on what you want, why you want it, and what the end result will be, the stronger your want-power will grow.

You are allowed to want what you want. You deserve to have what you want. I invite you to drop the forced willpower concept and play with boosting your want-power.

But only if you want to.

How many times a day do you let the words "I don't know" stop you from taking action or making a decision?

What should I do? I don't know.
What is my plan? I don't know.
How will I get this done? I don't know.
Who can help me? I don't know.

What if you couldn't use that answer? What if you used your curiosity and available resources and found an answer that would help you take the next step? WHAT IF YOU DID KNOW?

I invite you to experiment for the next few days with your IDK's. Every time you hear yourself say, "I don't know," immediately ask yourself, "But what if I DID know?" Be curious for an answer. Use your resources. Don't give up. Watch what happens.

You DO know!

When somebody does something that breaks the law or the rules, or acts in a way that generally feels like they have little disregard for you or anyone else, you may get frustrated or angry and say, "Wait! They can't do that!"

Ohhh, but they can. And they just did. Your reaction (and resistance) is what Byron Katie calls "fighting with reality." And, as she says, "When you fight with reality, you lose, but only 100% of the time."

Saying, "They can't do that!" will not stop their behavior. You don't get to choose what they do, but you can choose whether and how it affects you. Knowing what you will tolerate, setting and staying within strong boundaries, and following through with consequences will help you create a different and better reality for you. And you CAN do that!

There is so much more to you than you have learned to be. Explore yourself. Expand yourself. Empower yourself.

Before you negatively label somebody today, I invite you to first ask, "Is that who they are, or is that just how I'm seeing them?"

The same applies when you're labeling yourself. Q

Is there something you're forgetting to allow today? Are you allowing yourself to be patient? Laugh? Look at things differently? Forgive yourself or someone else? Relax? Are you allowing yourself to feel? Be wrong? Be right? Be confused? Be yourself?

Are you allowing yourself to be seen? Be real? Be loved? Love others? Be healed? Have fun?

I invite you to be a sculptor in the art of allowing. You'll be amazed by what you can create in your life.

The easiest and most assured way to feel imprisoned is to choose to make your decisions and take actions based on what other people think of you or what they think you should do.

I invite you to ask yourself, "Do I look good in stripes?"

There are no rules that will keep you from doing or not doing something in a certain way if you do not believe in the rules. Your beliefs are your rules. I invite you to review and reassess your own rules often. Some of the rules (beliefs) you've held for years may no longer be serving you.

There is more than one way to go about things.
There is more than one way to see things.
There is more than one way to heal, mend, and solve things.
There is more than one way to work and play.
There is more than one way to discover and learn and apply.
There is more than one way to meditate, pray, and worship.
There is more than one way to communicate.
There is more than one way to mourn, celebrate, and show love.

I invite you to choose the way that serves you best, and be open to the possibility that others do it another way. There's room for everyone and everything.

A tipping point is where a series of small changes or incidents become significant enough to cause a larger, more important change—also known as "something's gotta give."

You will know you've reached your tipping point when it becomes more uncomfortable to stay in the situation than to face the fear of changing it. 😮

If you're having a hard time figuring out what you want, it could be that you have some limiting beliefs about what you can have or what you deserve. If you don't think you can have it or deserve it, you may also be thinking that you can't or shouldn't want it or ask for it. And when you keep yourself from wanting or asking for something, you shut off the possibility of receiving.

I invite you to WANT WHAT YOU WANT, no matter what it is! Wanting has no limits or measure of deservedness. Then, open to the possibility of receiving, and allow the Universe to take it from there. 🎯

According to Google, the 2nd Edition of the 20-volume Oxford English Dictionary contains full entries for 171,476 words in current use and 47,156 obsolete words. To this may be added around 9,500 derivative words included as subentries.

It makes one wonder: with all those wonderful words, why do we constantly use "hard" to describe things that take effort in our lives?

What if we used different, more positive descriptive words? Doesn't it feel better to believe:

"I work very diligently to get what I want" instead of "I work so hard"?

"Eating healthy food is challenging for me" instead of "Dieting is hard"?

"It takes conscientious effort to communicate with them" instead of "Trying to make them understand is so hard"?

"There have been some unpleasant times in my life" instead of "My life has been so hard"?

The more you describe things as hard, the harder they become. I invite you to challenge yourself to find other words to relay your feelings. It's easy to make things hard. Why not make it easy to make things easier?

No amount of outside encouragement will make a difference in your success or happiness if you're not open to receive it from the inside. Self-compassion, self-forgiveness, self-love, and your belief in self-deservedness are the keys to opening the door to receive.

Offer help if it feels good to do so or if it is asked for and you want to help. Remember, though, that not everyone is here to be or wants to be fixed or rescued. Save your energy and enthusiasm for yourself and for those who want it. The others will find their way. Or they won't. Their path, not yours.

How much time does it take to be kind to yourself?
How much does it cost to believe you are worthy?
So small the investment.
So great the return.
Always a bull market.

Some people believe that courage and fearlessness are the same. Not true. Here's an example of how they are different.

Let's say you drive 65 miles per hour on the freeway every day without giving it a second thought. That's fearlessness. On the other hand, your neighbor is scared spitless to drive on the freeway. Yet, he knows that in order to get to his job and feed his family, the drive is essential. So every day, despite his fear, he chooses to make the drive. That's courage.

Courage is not the lack of fear but the decision that what is beyond the fear is worth going for and then choosing to go for it. 😮

Greed. Anger. Prejudice. Indecision. Stress. Control. Aggression. Addiction. Over-compensation. Co-dependency. All very clever disguises for fear.

If you're wearing one of these, I invite you take off the disguise and expose the fear for what it is. It's so much easier to work with what you can easily see. 🔴

"I'm missing out on that party."
"I'm missing out on knowing what's happening."
"I'm missing out on that job opportunity."
"I'm missing out on watching my kids grow up."

We often think we're missing out, when what's truly happening is that we're making choices to do something different, even when it feels like we have no choice—for example, when we say, "I have to stay home with the kids because I can't find a babysitter." Whether your choice is due to a sense of responsibility or generosity or it is led by guilt or ambition or any other feeling or reason, you are still making a choice.

I invite you take ownership of your choices. Instead of thinking that you're missing out, ask yourself, "Do I feel good about the what that I'm choosing (I love my kids and would never leave them alone, no matter what!)?"

There are a bazillion things happening every day. You're not missing out. You're making conscious choices.

Raising self-esteem doesn't happen overnight, and it truly does take practice. If you're not sure where to start, here's an exercise you can do: Every time a negative thought about yourself or your life enters your mind, name two positive thoughts to counteract it. Here are a couple of examples:

My hips are too wide:
1. My hips are sturdy.
2. I can walk perfectly with wide hips.

My job sucks:
1. My job is paying my bills right now.
2. My job does not define me.

You get the picture, right? The goal of this exercise is to avert your mind from the negative thoughts and open your mind and heart to the possibility that things are more positive than you are currently seeing them. Yes, it's simple. Yes, it's basic. And yes, it's effective if you allow it to be.

Feel free to name more than two counter-negative thoughts. What do you have to lose? (Now name two things you have to gain!)

If you want to make changes toward something different, I invite you to give yourself permission to allow it to feel different while it's happening.

Remember, different does not mean painful or uncomfortable—although it can if you want it to.

Money is often associated with success, and success is often associated with happiness. Yet, we all know of people who have more money than they could ever spend and still, they are not happy, so that negates the theory that money creates happiness.

The feeling of success can come from many places, not just money. I invite you to define what makes you feel successful that doesn't have a dollar amount associated with it. You may be surprised at how rich you really are.

Fear sets imaginary limitations. You can't know your real limitations if you don't give yourself permission to stretch beyond the fear to see what you're really capable of.

Just a side note: stretching may be uncomfortable, but only until it isn't. 😲

Every minute of every day of the year, you hold a wonderful gift.
From the minute you open your eyes.
At breakfast. In the shower. In the closet.
As you drive. At your job.
At every meeting. In every conversation.
At dinner. During TV time. As you lay your head down.

It's the gift that keeps on giving. The gift that never gets old.
The gift that's always appropriate. The gift that's always free.
The gift that guides your happiness.

Choice. The greatest gift of all. 🚩

What does "wrong" mean? As an adjective, it means "1. not correct or true, 2. unjust, dishonest or immoral." As an adverb, it means "in an unsuitable or undesirable manner or direction." As a noun it means "an unjust, dishonest or immoral action." As a verb it means "act unjustly or dishonestly toward (someone)."

Funny how "wrong" has become the unintended, negative go-to word we use when someone is feeling ill, acting irrationally, not joining in or voicing a differing opinion. We ask, "What is WRONG with you?" when we are actually searching for an answer to how they are feeling.

I invite you today to identify a word other than "wrong." Instead of asking what's wrong, why not ask, "What feels different?" or "What is bothering you?" Feel free to ask yourself the same questions if you have a habit of beating yourself up. There's nothing wrong with being more positive.

A tradition is:

> 1: an inherited, established, or customary pattern of thought or action
> 2: the handing down of beliefs and customs by word of mouth or by example without written instruction: also, a belief or custom thus handed down.

Basically, we do what we do because that's the way it's always been done.

I invite you look at your family traditions and ask yourself, "Is this tradition working for me—or am I just following the path of what I am supposed to believe or do, just because that's the way it's always been believed or done?" Also ask yourself, "Does following this tradition bring me joy or stress?"

Traditions can be great! And if they're not, you can always choose to end or change them to fit your beliefs and thoughts.

Have you ever attempted to quickly thread a needle, but the thread wouldn't go through? It's so frustrating! You have to stop what you're doing to go find your glasses. Once you put your glasses on, you notice that the thread is frayed on the end, so you take out your sharp scissors and trim it. Then, you try again with your glasses on, the thread just sails right through the eye of the needle, and you're able to go on with your sewing. Yay!

Yes. Metaphor. Slow down. Focus. Notice. Use your tools. Realize. Be happy. It's sew easy! Q

Not all people come into your life to stay forever. Not every person will become a close friend or lover. Some people you will know briefly, yet deeply. You will find some people hard to like or be around. Not all of them will like or love you. Yet, each person who crosses your path is here for a purpose or to teach you a precious lesson.

When the times comes to part ways for whatever reason, think about their true purpose in your life. What lessons did they teach you? How did they fulfill their role so you could grow?

We are blessed to have many teachers. I invite you to take the opportunity to learn from each of them. Acknowledge them. be grateful for whatever part they played on your journey, and continue on.

There are no dumb questions. There are, however, questions you may be asking to which you already, deep down, know the answer but are afraid to uproot.

Be brave. Dig deep. Be open. Allow. Denial rarely helps. 😮

"I don't know where to start and I don't want to make a wrong move." It's often the thought that keeps our most passionate dreams from becoming reality. If this feels familiar, I invite you to let go of the belief that everything has a defined beginning or a predetermined Step One.

Do something—anything—to move closer to your dreams. If it feels like you're starting in the middle, then the middle is where your start. It's possible that you'll need to move backward toward Step One to clean a few things up—or maybe not! At least you will be moving. And learning. And growing.

Wrong moves can't keep you from your dreams. Only no moves can. 🎯

Before you jump on somebody else's bandwagon, make sure they're playing your song. While the melody may be enticing, I invite you to listen closely to the words and meaning. Do you resonate with the tone? Does it feel like harmony to your soul? If not, it's okay to hop off and march to the beat of your own drum. 🚏

The Golden Rule is "Do unto others as you would have them do unto you." It's a noble and loving guideline. Unfortunately, there are some who interpret it to mean "Be kind and work hard for others" and they leave themselves out of the equation. That can lead to a couple of potential disasters:

> 1. They work hard to please others with the expectation that others will do the same to fill their happiness cup for them, which doesn't always happen and can lead to disappointment and resentment.
> 2. They work hard to please others with no expectation and neglect to fill their own happiness cup, which can lead to emptiness, unfulfillment, and exhaustion.

Either way, nobody's happiness cup is getting filled. I don't know about you, but neither way feels Golden to me.

If either of these scenarios is feeling true for you today, I invite you to tweak the Golden Rule a bit. As you "do unto others as you would have them do unto you," make sure you are "doing unto yourself" as much or more. That way, nobody's happiness cup goes empty.

Life becomes harder the minute you think it is.

The good news is the opposite is also true.

Good news is better. 🔍

Imagine the positive energy that would be created if the media and powers-that-be would sensationalize and publicize the good things happening in the world.

Seriously. Stop what you're doing right now, close your eyes, and imagine. Let's start a trend. 💭

If you will give yourself permission to focus on being in each day and opening to all the possibilities it has to offer, greeting and ending it with love and gratitude, you will soon find that your desire to know or control the future will no longer seem as important or relevant as it once did. And that will feel like freedom. 🔍

The key to learning the hard way? Just keep doing what isn't working.

When nothing changes, nothing changes. 💭

Is there something you're putting off until later? Something you know needs to be done or something you really want to get done? Yet somehow, you can't bring yourself to do it now?

What is the reason you're putting it off? If you're not really sure, there's most likely some underlying fear attached. It could be fear of confrontation, fear that you won't succeed or that you won't be good enough, fear that you won't know the next step, fear that you're wasting your time, or fear that you won't be able to afford it.

By now, you know you have a choice. You can either let fear stop you in your tracks and keep you from moving forward, or you can look at your situation through the eyes of love. You can ask yourself, "What do I really want?" "How do I want to feel?" "What's the worst that can happen?" and "What if I weren't afraid?" You can look at evidence of times when you've moved forward and it all worked out. And you can remember that you are strong, powerful, and always loved—this is just another part of the journey.

Tip: don't forget to thank your fear for reminding you of all the fabulous choices you have available to you. 😮

If it feels like people are repeatedly taking advantage of you in a certain area, I invite you to reflect on your boundaries. What works for you? What will you no longer tolerate? Have you communicated your boundaries, including the consequences, in a non-confrontational way? Have you acted within the integrity of your boundaries and carried out the consequences when needed?

It's not your job to fix what you perceive to be someone else's bad behavior. It's not your job to make them respect you. They have to choose to do that themselves—or not. However, when given clear boundaries and choices, you may be surprised how willingly and easily they comply. If they don't, you still stand within your integrity and self-respect. And, in the long run, isn't that what really matters? Q

When faced with a challenge, sometimes it's hard to fathom that stretching past the uncomfortable will bring us the results we want. It often keeps us from getting off the ground with what we want to do. When that happens, I invite you to envision the stages of a balloon:

- A balloon with no helium is limp. It may be comfortable, but it's going nowhere.
- A little helium in the balloon makes it bouncy and able to be rolled, but it won't get off the ground.
- As the balloon takes more helium, it stretches and stretches, feeling the expansion, until suddenly it lifts into the air and floats freely and easily. It's so happy that it forgets about the uncomfortable expansion and just enjoys the rest of the journey.

Expansion is not always comfortable, but it's an essential part of the journey. I invite you to make like a balloon today and stretch!

Your brain can talk your body into or out of just about anything, even when you've set the best intentions or made solid commitments. Perhaps it's because we've been raised to "think" our way through things instead of listening to our body when it's telling us what it needs. When our body is longing for exercise, but we think we don't have time or that it will hurt too much, we let our thinking win.

When our body is longing to rest but we think we need to work more hours or accomplish a few more things, we let our thinking win. When we attempt to lift just 10 more pounds or push through for just one more mile, but our body is wracked with pain, we let our thinking win. When we commit to a healthier diet but have just one more donut or drink or cigarette, we let our thinking win.

Your body speaks to you constantly. I invite you to tune in to its frequency and listen. Give your brain and your body the opportunity to communicate and cooperate, because if your brain is always winning, your body will eventually have to lose.

What do you think about that?

A surefire way never to miss an opportunity is never to stop looking for one.

Opportunity abounds when you are open to it.

It is said that patience is a virtue, but what does that mean? It means that patience, the ability to delay gratification and wait quietly for things to happen in their own time, is a good trait to have. And it is! Impatience often leads to irrational behavior and wasted energy when you try to force something to happen sooner than it is able. It is often a detriment to what you are trying to achieve.

While patience is a virtue, note that patience is often a challenging practice. It's more than just waiting, it's a stretching of the trust muscle. When you practice patience, you trust in the deliverance of Divine timing all for your greatest and highest good. I invite you to practice patience. It will be worth the wait.

Nice and kind do not always travel together. It is not uncommon for a person to appear to be nice, yet not act with genuine kindness. It is also not uncommon for a person to act with genuine kindness, yet appear not to be nice.

So ends another lesson from the school of Don't Judge a Book by its Cover.

Footnote: It is very common to simultaneously be both nice and kind. In fact, it's rather awesome.

Want a little pick-me-up to chant as you work, walk, drive, or whatever else you're doing? Try this mantra from Charles Haanel:

I AM WHOLE, PERFECT, STRONG, POWERFUL, LOVING, HARMONIOUS, AND HAPPY

Breathe deeply while repeating with belief a few times. Better than a triple-espresso latte, and caffeine-free!

J ust a friendly refresher:

When someone is unhappy, it is all about their choices and resistance.
When someone blames you for their unhappiness or wants to make you a part of their drama or wants you to change, it is all about their choices and resistance.

Likewise:

When you are unhappy, it is all about your choices and resistance.
When you blame someone else for your unhappiness or want to make them part of your drama or want them to change, it is all about your choices and resistance.

I'm glad we had this talk. +

W hile some decisions are more challenging than others, not making a choice is a choice. Deciding not to decide is always an option as well. "I have no choice" is rarely, if ever, a true statement. 🌧

Fear and doubt are the doors we open when we're convinced we don't know what to do. Possibility is the door we open when we detach from the thought that we should know what to do.

Which doors will you open today? 😮

If you're a golfer, you probably already know that if you loosen your grip on the club a bit, your ball will travel further and more freely. Grasping the club tightly restricts your movement and reduces the natural flow of your swing, which in turn causes you to have to take more frustrating swings in or order to reach the hole.

You know where I'm going with this, right?

I invite you to loosen your grip today and get into the natural flow. There's nothing like the feeling of a hole-in-one!

When you say, "I'm not ready," it usually means one of two things:

#1: You're moving forward with a process and things are lining up. It's a matter of patience and timing, and the goal is in sight. You're just not quite there.

#2: You're afraid to make a move.

If #1 is the reason you're not ready, YOU GO! Keep moving forward! You'll be there in no time!

If #2 is the reason you're not ready, I invite you to explore the heck out of that fear. Uncover the truth of it. Find help if you need it, and then get ready to move.

Are you ready for this? 😲

I'm often asked, "Why is the go-to answer always 'breathe'?"

Because when you're struggling, frustrated, angry, sad, depressed, or confused and you want to make a decision or a change, the fastest, easiest, and most effective path is through calm and clarity.

Breathing is the doorway to calm and clarity. Breathe, and open the door.

How do you get past resistance when you keep practicing the same old "but that will never happen" story?

Try this: after practicing your "but that will never happen" story, extend your story with "but if it DID happen..." and play the story out. For example, "My prince charming will never come, but if he DID show up, he would look like... and act like... and I would feel like..." or "I'll never have enough money to go on a fabulous vacation, but if I DID have the money, I would go to...and I would do...and it would feel like..."

See what we're doing here? We're giving resistance a run for its money just by imagining the possibilities. The more energy and practice you give to the possibilities, the more likely you are to give yourself permission to realize them.

It CAN happen. 🌀

When you are annoyed or frustrated, do you tend to choose the "bless-ed" side or the blessed side? For example:

"I'm sitting in this traffic jam and there's not a blessed thing I can do about it!"

or

"Even though I'll be late, I'm so blessed to be sitting in my air-conditioned car with my radio and my phone, totally safe from that accident."

When unfortunate things happen, I invite you to choose gratitude and remember that you are at all times blessed. It will all work out either way, but why not choose as much as possible to experience the blessed peace you long for?

In case you hadn't noticed, when you repress or deny things about yourself, they don't disappear. They just lay under the surface, waiting for the chance to do their teaching.

I invite you to explore and embrace your shadow-side. The sooner you understand and accept your whole self, the easier it will be to do the same with others.

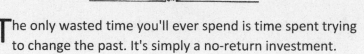

The only wasted time you'll ever spend is time spent trying to change the past. It's simply a no-return investment.

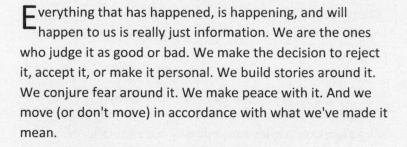

Everything that has happened, is happening, and will happen to us is really just information. We are the ones who judge it as good or bad. We make the decision to reject it, accept it, or make it personal. We build stories around it. We conjure fear around it. We make peace with it. And we move (or don't move) in accordance with what we've made it mean.

What are you making it all mean today? If you feel bad or uncomfortable, I invite you to step back and assess the information again. There is much to be discovered if you will give yourself permission to be open and objective.

Choosing to change your behavior so you'll feel better and be happier is self-empowerment.

Choosing to change your behavior so others will see the change in you still gives them the power.

Choose to change, live your truth, feel better, and be happy for YOU.

What were you taught about crying? Was it "Keep it to yourself!" "Man up!" "Big girls don't cry" or "There's no crying in baseball!" If you hold back your tears like a dam holds back water, keep in mind what happens when a dam breaks: it becomes a disaster area. The clean-up and healing can take months or years, and sometimes the damage is irreparable.

I invite you to open the flood gates and shamelessly let your tears flow. Unless, of course, you enjoy cleaning up after a disaster.

Worry is "planned fear." Instead of motivating us to take in-the-moment action the way real fear does, worry plans—and then waits for something bad to happen.

I invite you to remember that nothing is happening in the future. It's all happening right now. If you feel the need to make a plan, why not plan to be calm and confident that everything is going to be okay? It makes the waiting easier.

Are shiny objects stealing your focus? Ask yourself (and don't skip the answers):

Is this shiny object serving me?
Is this how I intended to spend my precious time today?
Would I sabotage someone else's mission?
Why am I willing to sabotage mine?
What am I afraid will happen if I focus?

Take your power back. Don't fear focus; make friends with it.

My intentions and goals matter to me.
I matter to me.
It's only shiny if I let it be.
It's only hard if I think it is.
Focus is my friend.

You receive valuable information for every "Well, that didn't go so well" event and every "Wow, that went *really* well!" event that occurs.

What will you do with this precious information today?

Your mind is on automatic in so many areas. Think about all the actions you take the very same way every time: brushing your teeth, tying your shoes, locking the door, making coffee, feeding the dog... These actions become routine because they work for you. No need to recreate the wheel every day—just do it the same way. Convenient. Easy. Comfortable. But, what if things were suddenly different and no longer routine? What if you lost the use of a hand? Would you stop brushing your teeth, feeding the dog, and so on? My guess is that the answer is no. You'd assess what no longer works and adjust to a new way that works with your new circumstances.

The same thing happens with our automatic thoughts. "When I see/hear (this), I automatically think (this)." Unfortunately, automatic isn't always convenient, easy, or comfortable. If you have automatic thoughts that make you feel defensive, judgmental, stressed, angry, or depressed, I invite you to take a time-out to assess them. Do you believe the thoughts? Or are they just part of your routine? If you're not completely comfortable with a thought, or it doesn't seem to be serving you, what adjustment can you make in your thinking to change it?

Automatic and routine are good when they're working. Don't be afraid to make needed adjustments when they are not.

There is always a peaceful alternative to conflict. As you think about the various scenarios and their possible outcomes, which of them brings you the greatest feeling of peace in your mind and body? That's the one to choose.

Imagine how much easier your life could be if you could let go of struggling with the illusion that it should be different.

Remember that time you put on that jacket you hadn't worn in a while, and you found a $10 bill in it? What a pleasant surprise!

Remember when you received that rebate check in the mail that you forgot you even applied for? So cool!

Remember that extra dollar you donated at the grocery store for that charity? Feeling generous!

Remember making that last payment on your loan? So satisfying!

If you're feeling stressed about money, I invite you to stop and think of all the times money felt good and easy. Change your vibration to something more attractive. There is no reason to believe financial abundance won't happen again.

Be care-full what you wish for.
(See what we did there?)

One of the many benefits of not concerning yourself with what other people think is all the extra time you'll save not feeling the need to defend or explain yourself.

When you know what works for you,
When you are confident in your truth,
When you are steadfast in your boundaries,
When you stay in your own business,
There is no need to defend.

When you find yourself negatively fast-forwarding to the future and comparing the worst-case scenario to a challenge you're currently experiencing, or making up stories about what other people are going to say or how they will react and building more fear that causes you anxiety, panic, and confusion, I invite you to stop the spiraling madness by asking yourself this question:

"What are the best possible outcomes?"

Give yourself permission to be open to the possibility that things can be different than what you're projecting them to be. 😮

Would you hail a taxi, get in, and then sit there, expecting the driver to know where you want to go? My guess is probably not. So why do it with your life?

Be clear about what you want and ask for it. That's what the driver—the Universe—needs in order to give it to you.

The first and best tool you have in any situation is CHOICE. You can't always choose the situation, but you can always choose how you react, act, and feel.

Make good choices.

If you are in the teaching position (and, by the way, you almost always are), I invite you to let go of the outcome of your lesson. The student will get it in time—or they won't. (And by "teacher" and "student," I mean you and everyone else in the world.)

Many live in fear of contracting some dreaded disease or random floating germ that will affect their wellbeing, forgetting that what we focus on is what we get.

A better way to live might be to choose to focus on how healthy you feel or have felt in the past. Thank your body from your head to your toes for all of its support. Live in gratefulness for being able to breathe and think and feel instead of fearing that those opportunities will be taken away.

Warning: Side effects include frequent smiling attacks, which are highly contagious. 😮

It's been said that "freedom comes with a cost," yet freedom seems to be the number one desire on everyone's want list. So, what is the cost of freedom?

- Honesty and truthfulness—to yourself and others
- Living within the boundaries of your values and integrity
- Releasing the binds of caring what others think
- Letting go of shoulds, need-tos, and worries
- Living in the moment instead of the past or the future
- Acceptance and appreciation for the diversity of all others and things

I don't know about you, but the cost seems more than reasonable in exchange for the bounty of the return.

What are you willing to pay for your freedom?

It is said that smoking is a hard habit to break, that daily exercise is a good habit to have, and that meditation is a challenging habit to form.

A habit is something we practice so repetitively that it becomes an embedded and automatic thought or action process. In other words, we do it because that's what we've trained ourselves to do. Some of our habits serve us better than others. Some of our habits even cause us suffering.

As you go about your day, I invite you to observe how many things you think or do out of habit, and ask yourself, "How is this habit serving me? Is it a habit I'd like to change?"

If your intention is to change your habit, remember that change happens when we practice something different. You simply have to choose the "something different" that serves you and practice it.

You already know how to practice. Take the first step and repeat. ◎

The thing about drama is, you always get to choose whether or not to participate. Sure, you may unexpectedly get sucked into the center-stage position from time to time, but if it's not the part you want to play, you don't have to open your mouth or act. Though the script may seem enticing, even starving actors know when the part isn't worth taking.

I invite you to choose the parts you want to play in this show called LIFE.

Impossible things are done every day. Discoveries, inventions, creations, healing, rescues, recoveries, enlightenment, forgiveness, breakthroughs, and records broken that did not seem possible at first.

Nothing is impossible unless you believe it is.
And nothing is possible unless you believe it is.

Imagine the possibilities.

Life isn't fair—and it's not supposed to be. Life is filled with contrast, because without contrast we would not be inspired or motivated to move forward or create anything new or positive. If life were fair and everything were equal, one person's negative experience would be everyone's negative experience. One person's illness would be everyone's illness. One person's poverty would be everyone's poverty.

If there's one thing that is fair, it's that everyone has choices. I invite you to look at life's contrast as a great blessing. Choose to take the opportunities presented to you, and move toward what feels good for you.

Life treats you as you see it. Life says, "I'll be whatever you want me to be." If you see life as a problem, life will be a problem for you. If you see life as an obstacle to get over, obstacles will appear for you to solve. Conversely, if you see life as blessings or miracles, life will treat you with blessings and miracles.

All you have to do to answer the question, "How's life treating you?" is take a look at how you're looking at life. Perhaps a more productive question would be, "How am I treating life?"

We've all heard stories of the heroes who lift cars off of people crushed underneath them or charge into burning buildings and rescue fire victims. How do they do that?! Adrenaline certainly plays a part, but what most certainly doesn't happen is the taking of time for fear or doubt. The unsuspecting hero doesn't stand there and say, "Gee. I could never lift that car. What if I try and fail? What if I look stupid? I'm not fully prepared for this. Maybe I should wait..." No. They put fear and doubt aside and immediately get to the task at hand. Because that's what heroes do.

Why is it then, when under much MUCH less pressure, we stop and entertain our fears and doubts before getting to the task at hand?

I invite you to be your own hero today. Rescue yourself from your own fears and doubts. Because that's what heroes do.

How much do you want to break a bad habit? How much do you want to create a better way for yourself? How much do you want things to change? How many times will you give in to your "just this one last time" thinking? Because every single "just this one last time" thought is an indicator that you're not quite committed.

What do you really want? What are you willing to do or not do to achieve it? What discomfort are you willing to endure or push through in order to get it?

Whatever IT is, it awaits you beyond the "just this one last time" point, not before.

Your reality is what you believe it is. Another's reality is what they believe it is. The two realities are not always the same.

When you make a judgment that another should "face reality," what you are meaning is that "they should face my reality" (or the reality as the group or majority sees it).

And when you say, "They should," *your* reality is that you are not in your own business.

We've grown up with the notion that mistakes are bad. Since nobody wants to be associated with "bad," we are motivated not to make mistakes. Unfortunately, this type of thought and behavior can lead to anxiety-filled perfectionism, control issues, and plain old fear of making a decision, all of which keep us from moving forward and living life to its fullest potential.

I invite you to consider the possibility that there are no mistakes, just choices that create experiences. And through these experiences, we make more choices based on how we feel about our previous experiences. It would make sense, therefore, that we'd have experiences that feel less perfect than others, because if all our experiences were absolutely perfect, why would we choose to move to the next experience?

There are no mistakes. 😮

Let's play a game of 20 excuses. Of the list below, cross off all the excuses you've used in the past year. Then, put an X by the ones you cross off that you've used in the past month.

Too tired
Too scared
Too embarrassed
Too expensive
Too late
Too early
Too self-conscious
Takes too long/not enough time
Too much work
Can't get motivated
Too busy
Too depressed
Too hard
Too hungry
Too visible/showy
Too boring
Too cold
Too hot
Too far
Too overwhelming

What does your list look like? Lots crossed out? Good! Excuses are the power-suckers of life. So, since you've crossed them off the list, why not cross the out of your life? And the ones you put an X by? Well, X stands for "kiss," so you can kiss them goodbye first! You can do it—no excuses!

Here's a 20-second intentional gift challenge:

When you're sitting in traffic, give yourself 20 seconds to intentionally listen to the words and music on your radio. Enjoy the entertainment as if it were playing just for you!

When you're sitting in a restaurant or having a meal, take 20 seconds to intentionally breathe in the delicious aromas of the food. Notice how they light up your senses with anticipation. Then, enjoy every bite!

When you're hurrying through the mall, your office, or your home, take 20 seconds to stop and intentionally notice the furnishings and feel the joy they were meant to bring.

If you see someone struggling, sad, or confused, take 20 seconds and intentionally send an outpouring of love straight from your heart to theirs.

Give yourself these small gifts and intentionally receive their great magic.

The quickest way to get out of an unwanted situation is to first fully accept that you are in one.

Denial = delay.

When in resistance of doing something we have fear around, we often fall into what I call "dung beetling." We take a little piece of crap (the fearful thought), and we roll it into an insurmountable ball of poo (using excuses, denial, and avoidance) that we push in front of us (focus on) to the point where we can no longer see what it is we really want or where it is we want to go.

It's time to cut the crap. I invite you to focus on what it is you really want (I'm pretty sure it's not an "insurmountable ball of poo"). You may still have fear, but you don't have to make it bigger than it really is.

How are you going to roll today?

L ao Tzu said:
If you are depressed, you are living in the past.
If you are anxious, you are living in the future.
If you are at peace, you are living in the present.

Where are you choosing to live today?

A ll the Nitro Cold Brew, 5-Hour Energy, or Red Bull in the
world won't solve the problem if you keep over-
committing. Just because you're awake doesn't mean you're
connected and fully functioning.

I invite you to be mindful of how you are committing your
time and energy. It doesn't all have to be done, and you don't
have to be the one to do all of it. Move with intention, and
listen to your body when it tells you to rest.

Alexander Graham Bell had a wild dream, and—after many failures—eventually invented and patented the first practical telephone in 1876. In 1976, 97 years later, Motorola had a wild dream, and—after many failures—produced the first hand-held mobile phone. In 2007, 34 years after that, Apple had yet another wild dream, and—after many failures—produced a handheld phone that was also a computer.

Today—after many, many failures—we can wear a watch that lets us communicate around the world, control our car, track our fitness, play music, discover the weather, and more. All of this because somebody had a wild dream and pursued it, letting nothing—especially multiple failures—stop them.

The things we take for granted today were once somebody's wildest dream, and the process of realizing that dream included multiple failures. What is your wildest dream, and what's keeping you from it? I hope it isn't fear of failure. 😮

ABCs. Counting. Colors. Reading. Growing up, we learn so many things we use every day and that serve us our entire lives. And, we learn so many things we use every day that *don't* serve us:

- Don't get too big for your britches.
- Don't be selfish.
- We can't afford that.
- Good girls and boys don't dress/act/talk that way.
- Don't question authority.
- You're a dreamer. Dreamers are not successful.
- Don't break the rules.
- This is how you SHOULD act/think/feel.

For many people, these and other beliefs are as ingrained as the alphabet and 2+2=4. Unfortunately, these learned beliefs are the ones that keep us from moving forward. They make us feel like we're 12 years old. They keep us playing small.

When you feel like you're holding back and playing small, I invite you to remember that YOU ARE NO LONGER 12 YEARS OLD. You do not have to believe everything you've been told. You have the power to question what works for you and what you truly believe. Give yourself permission to unlearn the things that no longer serve you. Be your own teacher.

Following your heart is not always easy or comfortable. Neither is living in your truth or walking through fear.

But it is always worth it. You can do this.

You can. 😮

Of all the powers you possess, being able to change the way another person acts, thinks, or feels is not one of them. The good news is that nobody else has that power over you, either. The other piece of good news is that you do possess the power of influence, and influence is the catalyst of the greatest superpower of all: CHOICE.

I invite you to summon your power of influence with love and for the good of all mankind so we all can make good choices, because choice leads to change. ⌐

There's one intention that covers everything:

"I will make choices that are in my best and highest good, that move me in the direction of what I really want and the way I want to feel."

That should do it! 🎯

What is the reason you're not asking for what you want?

Is it because, if you get what you want, you'll have to make a move in that direction? That could be scary.

Is it because, if you don't get what you want, you'll have to make a move in a different direction? That could be scary too.

Is it because the simple act of asking for what you want will mean you will get an answer, and then you'll actually have to make a move? Even scarier.

Have you noticed that all of this "not asking" is keeping you immobilized? Scariest ever!

Ask the questions and get moving. 😮

Control of and rule over anything other than one's self and true peace cannot coexist, for true peace need not and cannot be controlled.

Be the true peace you seek.

We often set rules and boundaries around ourselves because we're afraid we're not going to get what we want, or because we're afraid we're going to get something we don't want. This is a reminder that if your rules and boundaries are based on fear, you are in a state of resistance, and if you are in a state of resistance, it's more challenging for the Universe to deliver and, therefore, more challenging for you to receive what it is you want.

I invite you to set intentional guidelines to follow instead of fear-based rules, and set self-love-based boundaries for you to live within instead of fear-based boundaries to keep others out.

Fear controls. Love flows. Which feels better to you?

Oftentimes, the reason we suffer is that we believe others cannot handle our truth.

Just a reminder: you never get to decide what another can or cannot handle. You DO get to decide how much and for how long you will suffer. ◎

Guilt is a taught response, either openly or subliminally. It's the message that you should feel bad for not doing or wanting something that would benefit another's agenda or expectations. Guilt involves shame and dirty pain. It's a feeling of "less than." Guilt aims to drain your power and render you submissive. If you are having feelings of guilt, they are most likely not serving you well.

I invite you to bathe yourself in personal boundaries, confidence in your own choices, and complete love and respect for yourself, for these are guilt's greatest repellants. In fact, take a long soak. ⬤

Embarrassment is one of the emotions we feel when we think we're being judged by others. Embarrassment is a by-product of the shame we feel around the rules we've been taught to believe and the unrealistic standards we've been taught to hold regarding how we should appear in the world compared with the way our life is or the way we want it to be.

Since we never get to choose what other people think about us, I invite you to let that sh*t go. I also invite you to shift your embarrassed or shameful thought to one that takes the current reality in account. "This is the way it is right now, and I'm working to change it" or "This is the way it is right now, and it does not define me."

Life is full of opportunity. Feeling embarrassed is just another opportunity to grow.

Ever been in one of the situations where you've tried and tried, pushed and pulled, argued, begged, pleaded, threatened, promised, ranted, cried, and tried some more and still nothing worked—only to find that the minute you threw your hands in the air and gave up trying to control the situation, everything magically started coming together?

Behold the power of letting go of control.

May the non-force be with you.

If you're wanting to make real change(s) for yourself in the coming year, I invite you to ask yourself AND ANSWER these probing questions before you set your resolutions or intentions, especially if you've failed to carry them out in the past.

> 1. What is the underlying reason I want/don't want this? (Hint: It's a feeling that you're seeking.)
> 2. On a scale of 1-10, how passionate and positive am I about it?
> 3. What (if anything) has kept me from it in the past? (What are my fears and excuses?)
> 4. What am I now willing to give up or change to have this that I wasn't willing to give up or change in the past?
> 5. Where/to whom can I go to for help/support/inspiration to stay on track?

Honest answers to these questions will help you determine and move toward the changes you want to make. 🎯

Of course, you can learn from their mistakes!

Look around you. Every day, fellow humans are teaching you things that you cannot learn from books or school through their various thoughts, actions, and energies. They are offering you endless opportunities to choose what works for you, no matter how or if it works for them. It's when you choose the opposite of what works for you that you get to learn from your mistakes.

We've all had big visions and set big goals. We think that reaching them is the pinnacle on which we can stand and finally be happy. We work hard, and sometimes we reach them. Often, we give up. Why? Because we forget to recognize the small wins along the way. Those tiny success steps that allow us to take the next one. The steps that lead us to the pinnacle and remind us of how far we've come and how much we've accomplished.

I invite you to celebrate each small victory as you make each step. Be grateful for ALL you've accomplished. Recognize your greatness. Why wait? Get that feeling of reaching the pinnacle NOW! You are AMAZING! Q

When you don't allow yourself to specifically envision something good happening in your life because you don't want to set yourself up for disappointment, you are closing the door to any possibility of receiving that specific something.

And the funny thing is, when you "protect yourself" from being disappointed, you are actually not only envisioning disappointment, you are already living it.

Manifesting works both ways. 🎯

New Year's Day is that magical day whereupon people vow to begin the miraculous transformation of their lives that they've been putting off all year.

The truth is, January 1st merely marks the beginning of a new year on the Gregorian calendar. The day doesn't magically change your mindset. It can't dissolve your limiting beliefs. It won't lift your butt off the couch, take the fork out of your mouth, look for that new job, reduce your credit card balance, make you act with more kindness, or work on that relationship. You still have to do all of that yourself. And you can start ANY DAY OF THE YEAR.

The magic is in you, not the day. What are you waiting for?

Ever find yourself on the edge of an unwanted argument where you're being accused by the other person of telling them they're wrong? Here is some non-confrontational/non-blaming language you can use when you simply don't see eye-to-eye:

"I'm not saying you're wrong, I'm saying...":
- I don't agree with you
- I don't understand
- It doesn't work for me
- I see it differently
- I'd like to know the facts
- I'm unfamiliar with it

By stating only how *you* feel and what *you* believe, and by not using the word "you" in your response, there is nothing for the accuser to defend. Unfortunately, it doesn't mean they won't continue to provoke you to engage in a battle. If they do, pull out the one "you" statement that may finally shut them down: "You may be right."

Is it money you want, or is it the feeling of freedom?
Is it money you want, or is it the feeling of security?
Is it money you want, or is it the feeling of power?
Is it money you want, or is it the feeling of adventure?
Is it money you want, or is it the feeling of abundance?
Is it money you want, or is it the feeling of expansion?

Money is merely printed paper, metal, and numbers on a bank statement or stock certificate upon which we place value. You could sit on a pile of actual money and still not feel free, secure, powerful, adventurous, abundant, or expansive.

What do you think would happen if you intentionally created and held those feelings in other areas of your life without attaching their value to money? I can't be certain, but my guess is that money would come more easily to you. Imagine that: feeling great first, then having money. Q

Go ahead and resist your truth for as long as you want. It will usually wait patiently for you while you decide to quit suffering. Usually. Then again, sometimes it just wants to be known now. Can you live with the pressure?

What have you been wanting to do or change for a very long time? Perhaps start a business, leave a job, commit to a relationship (or leave one), quit smoking or drinking, start taking care of your health, or focus on your financial situation? Maybe you've made steps toward it, but you've fallen backward out of fear that you're not ready. How will you know when you're ready?

You will be ready to do what it takes to make the change when the discomfort of NOT changing outweighs the fear of changing.

Here's the thing, though: you don't have to wait for that tipping point! Suffering is a sign that change is an option and it's on the horizon. You get to choose your level of suffering.

Instead of wondering, "How will I know I'm ready?" I invite you to ask yourself, "How much suffering am I willing to tolerate?" I hope your answer is NONE, but it's your choice.

What if instead of telling yourself that "it's going to be hard" and automatically setting it up to feel hard, you tell yourself that "it's going to be different"? Then, you are at least open to the possibility of it not feeling hard instead of predetermining that it will be.

Your parents may have said, "You learned to walk when you were eight months old," when actually, the learning process started much earlier. You watched others walk. You rolled over, crawled, got up on your knees, and stood while holding onto something. You observed, you built your muscles, you found your balance, and you most likely fell many times before you walked. Then, when everything lined up just right, you started walking. It didn't magically happen in one day.

During the process, you didn't throw your hands in the air and declare, "I'll never be able to walk!" and then give up, did you? Thankfully not. Today, you don't even think about the process it took and how challenging it was. You simply and confidently walk where you want to go.

I invite you to remember that everything has a learning process that usually involves observing, building your skills, balancing your energy, and maybe even failing before it (whatever it is) "happens." As a child, you knew not to give up. Don't let the wiser, more experienced you give up now.

Q

Have you ever been close to what appears to be an intense, abstract painting that spectators were fawning over, and though you looked very hard, you just couldn't see what they were seeing? Maybe you became frustrated as you struggled to make sense of it. Maybe a wise spectator tapped you on the shoulder and suggested that you step back, soften your focus, and take a broader look. Then BAM! There it was. A beautiful, peaceful, perfect image of what the painter set out to accomplish.

Just a reminder that when things start to feel close, intense, and abstract, it helps to step back, soften your focus, and take a broader look to see the bigger picture of the beautiful, peaceful, perfect life you are creating.

BAM!

Meditation is a practice of being, not a practice of doing. Maybe that's why so many avoid meditation or say they can't meditate.

Whenever you feel like you're going backward, stop and take a good look around. Most likely you missed something pretty important. Once you find it and give it your attention, you can start moving forward again.

Whoop, there it is! 🔍

You don't need to tell your every truth to everyone—or anyone—in order to maintain a happy life. However, keeping deep, dark secrets inside you is like hosting slow acting, debilitating poison. Some of the toxic symptoms are guilt, shame, and self-loathing, and they manifest in various ways in your outside world. You may experience health issues like chronic weight gain or loss, stress, high blood pressure, sleep deprivation, or depression, to name a few.

Behaviors like people-pleasing, perfectionism, avoidance, addiction, overreacting, overcompensating, and paranoia may start to show up, and you may notice that your relationship connections are not as strong or as authentic as you would like them to be. Hiding these deep, dark secrets allows the inner poisoning to continue. Revealing your truth makes it much harder for the poison to spread and further harm you and those you love.

If you are experiencing the poison of keeping deep, dark secrets, I invite you to reveal them to someone you trust: a friend, loved one, advisor, counselor, minister, coach, or complete stranger. It may feel difficult, but remember, healing cannot fully start until the contaminate has been exposed to the light. 😮

If you're craving connection, longing to be more in-the-moment and wanting to consciously raise your vibration, I invite you to be specific with the way you communicate your gratitude. Instead of a brief, thank you (or no thank you at all), take the extra time and effort to express what you are grateful for and why. For example:

- Thank you for being on time for our meeting. It really helps my day flow more easily and I appreciate your help with that.
- Thank you for listening to me. I feel heard by you.
- Thank you for doing _____ . I feel honored by your actions.
- Thank you for your kind words. I feel your support.
- Thank you for the compliment. I feel loved and appreciated.

Bonus: Not only are you more closely connecting, being more in-the-moment and consciously raising your vibration, you're also giving the person you're thanking the opportunity to do the same without their even knowing! 🎯

While you're waiting for your big ship to come in, you don't have to spend all your time on the same dock. There are smaller boats that come by every day that will take you to the next landing, and additional small boats at that landing to take you to the next. Before you know it, you'll be meeting your big ship instead of waiting, waiting, waiting for it.

Why is it we're baffled when it appears that some kindergartners act more maturely than some CEOs and some octogenarians understand less about love than some teenagers? Perhaps it's because we've been taught to measure a persons' age in human years and we forget that their soul age is measured in lifetimes of experiences and lessons learned.

I invite you to consider the concept that this isn't the first rodeo for any of us, and that no matter what age we appear on earth, some of us have been riding through time much longer than others.

It gives the term "old soul" more merit now, doesn't it?

You have issues, you say? Trust issues. Commitment issues. Self-esteem issues. Co-dependent issues. Addiction issues. Faith issues. Relationship issues. Anger issues. Family issues. Money issues. Guilt issues. Shame issues. Enablement issues. Abandonment issues. Of course, the list of internal controversies goes on and on. Issues are battles with yourself that you fight in your own mind.

What if you looked at your issues from another angle? What if you saw every inner battle not as an issue but as an opportunity to grow in that area? An opportunity to choose differently or try something new? To see it no longer as a battle ground but as an experimental learning, growing, and choosing ground?

I invite you to give yourself permission to let go of the stories and entrapment of your issues and to look at the opportunities the Universe is providing to help you get to that place you really want to be. Yes, it may feel like work. But would you rather work for yourself or battle against yourself?

It's much more challenging to find your answers when you're avoiding the important questions.

Be brave. Boldly go. 😮

Picture yourself standing in front of an enormous and elaborate buffet where you can have anything you want to eat on the table.

While you're filling your plate, do you stop in front of everything you don't like and complain about how awful it is? Say that it shouldn't be on the table? Moan that it's ruining your life? That you can't move forward because it's still there in front of you? Or, do you simply skip past it because there are so many other deliciously pleasing treats to choose from?

I invite you to start thinking of life as an enormous and elaborate buffet table. You can choose to fill your plate with things that delight you and feed your soul, or you can focus on the things that don't—and go hungry. 🔍

Imagine how your day would feel if you allowed things (people and/or situations) to be different instead of believing they need to be categorized and placed in tight boxes of right or wrong, good or bad.

Do the words freedom, peaceful, relaxed, and unburdened come to mind? They do for me too.

If you were to compare the way you currently spend your days to being in college, trying to complete your degree, are these the classes you're taking right now?

- Facebook/Snapchat/Instagram 101
- How to stay engaged in family's and friends' drama
- Immediate response to insignificant email
- How to suck up your time with Netflix, Hulu, and Amazon Prime
- What's in your refrigerator now that wasn't there five minutes ago?

If so, you're definitely majoring in minor subjects at the University of Avoidance.

The good news is, today starts a brand-new semester and there's still time to change your major and transfer classes! 🔵

There's bound to be something or someone who trips one of your wires as you move through your day. Instead of blowing it up into something big and moving immediately into a negative vibe, I challenge you to keep it small and move immediately into a positive vibe:

It's just a flat tire. It could have been way worse. I'm very grateful that most days my tires are not flat and that they keep me safe and moving freely. No big deal.
I missed an appointment. So what? I'm human and it happens. I'm proud of myself for all the appointments I haven't missed. The world will keep turning. No big deal.
He's acting like a jerk. I'm so glad I have boundaries and I can choose not to take his behavior personally. I hope his life gets better because I KNOW mine will. No big deal.

By keeping it small, you keep your own vibration high and you manifest more of what you do want. Then life feels and gets better and better. Are you up for the challenge? It's really no big deal. 🚩

We are all human, and we are all seeking happiness and love in our own individual and varied ways. Some speak freely and openly, while others are quiet and more guarded with their words and emotions. Some are risk takers and front runners, while others are observers and followers.

There is no right or wrong way of being. There is only different.

When we remember and honor this simple piece of information, the doors of cooperation, collaboration, acceptance, allowing, and forgiveness open wide. Q

"I don't have time." "There's never enough time." "I ran out of time." None of these statements is ever true. Like air, time is ever-present for everyone. The hands on the clock do not stop, and the days and years on the calendar continue to pass no matter the level of our action or inaction.

In invite you to make friends with time. Stop blaming time as if it were making your choices for you. Time is always there for you. How you choose to utilize time is always up to you.

Do vision boards work? Does positive visualization work? Does looking for the silver lining in every situation work? The mere presence of these questions in your mind indicates that you want to feel better than the way you currently feel. You want more good things. Your inner being—and most likely your outer being as well—wants to feel good, and you want to know how to get there.

Let me ask you this: has complaining been working for you? Have thoughts of doubt and lack and fear been working for you? Has holding on to painful thoughts or repeating your story of what you don't want been working for you? My guess is that those thoughts and actions have only perpetuated those feelings or even made you feel worse.

The Law of Attraction states, "That which is like unto itself is drawn." In other words, positive thoughts and vibrations attract positive, and negative thoughts and vibrations attract negative.

If you want to feel better, vision boards, visualization, and silver-lining thinking help you get there. If you want to stay unhappy, complaining, thoughts of doubt, lack and fear, and holding on to painful thoughts and repeating painful stories will keep you where you are.

Your future is in your hands. Are you ready for a change?

When you are trying so hard to accomplish something but it feels like you are banging your head against a brick wall, I invite you to stop, step back, and ask the wall why it is there.

It's so much easier to hear the answer when there's not so much banging.

"Please be responsible for the energy you bring into this space."

You've read that before, right? It's about choosing how you show up for yourself and for others. It is about choosing your vibration, wherever you go. Because what you put out is what you get back.

Just a reminder: your body is the space you are always in. If you are bringing it negative thoughts of lack and unease, it will respond in kind.

I invite you to vibrate responsibly.

The word "but" has several defined meanings:
...except for the fact that
...no doubt
...without the certainty
...on the contrary
...yet
...with the exception of

We use "but" daily in at least one of these various contexts, AND we've also learned to use it as a defense for our fear-based excuses. "But I can't...." "But she won't..." "But I don't have..." "But they won't let me...."

I invite you to look at your "buts" today. Every time you say or think "but," ask yourself if you're defending a fear or excuse. Explore it. It's possible, and dare I say probable, that you can make forward progress if you become aware that what's stopping you is just your big but. 😮

What if you took a quick second or more to stop and feel what you are hearing?

Instead of being distracted by what you are doing or thinking.

Instead of preparing your rebuttal.

Instead of trying to prove you're right or making your opinion known.

Instead of going into "solve it" mode.

Instead of pacifying the speaker.

What if you let your heart listen before you allowed your mouth to respond?

And what if people did the same for you?

The very best and most effective way of letting people know that their negative opinions about you are not going to stop you from saying what you say, doing what you do, and being who you are...

is to keep saying what you say, doing what you do, and being who you are.

Stay in YOUR business.

The magical effect of you making it less important to yourself that people like you and more important that you like yourself is that people truly come to like you. Abracadabra!

If you find yourself too busy to sit down and contemplate your intention for the day, but still want to honor your practice, try this temporary shortcut:

1. Ask yourself how you're currently feeling or acting.
2. Ask yourself how you want to feel or act.
3. Pick two words to describe the action needed to get you there.

For example:

- If you feel hurried or overwhelmed, you might pick "SLOW DOWN"
- If you feel unheard or left out, you might pick "SPEAK UP"
- If you feel impatient and irritated, you might pick "BE PATIENT"
- If you are caught in someone else's theatrics, you might pick "NO DRAMA"

Pick two powerful words that will snap your awareness back to how you want to feel or act. Then, write them on sticky notes, a postcard, your mirror, your hand, your desktop, or wherever you will see them multiple times during the day. You'll be surprised how a little two-word reminder can turn your day around.

TRY IT. 🎯

World peace is improbable simply because there are so many people who want different things and have different beliefs. Fortunately, we all have the ability and power to achieve inner peace every day of our lives. And if you'll tap into that, the rest of the world will become much more tolerable, and indeed, more peaceful.

Imagine booking a rafting trip on an easy-flowing river. The bus drops you off at the perfect launching spot, where your guide has assured you that at the end of your awesome downstream experience a huge picnic awaits with great food, celebration, and fun surprises. You've talked to many people who have already made this beautiful trip and highly recommend it, and now you are so excited that you can't wait to get started. But once you get into your raft, you panic. What if this is hard? What if you do it wrong? What if you don't know what to do? You immediately turn your raft around and start paddling upstream. You fight the current because you can't see the picnic grounds and can't be sure they're really there. What if they're not? The river keeps moving and you keep struggling to stay where you are, because at the very least, it's familiar. However, you realize that it's hard to stay where you are, and it's becoming more and more frustrating and exhausting to try.

Sound familiar? If so, I invite you to put down your paddle and trust the flow. You have evidence of ease, reward, and joy. You have evidence that struggling is unpleasant and unproductive. Trust the flow. Nothing you want is upstream.

Q

Not living in your own truth is like wearing a pair of Louboutin heels that are two sizes too small. To the outside world, you look incredible! But, after a while, each step you take brings a little more friction and pain, until you find it harder and harder to keep your balance and move forward, especially when you're walking a rocky road.

I invite you to consider the proverbial shoes you put on each day. It's always your choice whether you would rather look good to the outside world or feel comfort and ease on your path.

Truth be told, the outside world is more likely looking at your heart than your feet.

The dictionary defines willpower as "control exerted to do something or restrain impulses." Wow. Those words feel negative, controlling, and full of resistance, don't they? "I won't eat that bad food because I don't want to be fat!" "I won't buy that outfit because I don't want to be poor!" "I won't smoke that cigarette because I don't want to get sick!" It's the double negative approach—pushing against what you don't want. Feels more like won't-power than willpower.

What if you dropped the idea of willpower and went with right-now power instead? Right-now power is self-intended, in-your-face decision making that empowers you to choose to move immediately toward what you desire. "I choose right now to honor my body with good food, because I want to feel more fit and healthy right now." "I choose to save my money right now because I want to feel financially secure and abundant right now." "I choose to pass on the cigarette right now because I want my lungs to feel clean and restored right now."

Empowering yourself to choose to do good for yourself is the double positive approach that allows you to feel good about yourself immediately. And it feels so much easier than pushing against what you don't want.

Of course, knowing what you DO want makes it even easier. Double up on the good. 🎯

To understand means to grasp mentally; to comprehend. To accept means to believe or come to recognize as valid or correct.

When you're having an "I get it mentally, I just don't think it should be happening" moment, you're experiencing the difference between understanding and accepting.
There is opportunity for growth within the difference.

Complaining is most useful when you're miserable and you want to stay that way.

Here's the bad news: no amount of evidence in the world can make something true or real for you if you don't believe it.

Now the good news: no amount of evidence in the world can make something true or real for you if you don't believe it.

Uh-huh. Don't stop believing the good stuff. 🔍

Short term convenience is not a precursor to long-term ease.

In other words, do all of that which you know must be done in order to achieve all of that which you really want.

It's not only possible but highly probable that you will have someone in your life whom you love very much AND of whom you are not very tolerant. They are there for a reason and have something to teach you. It could be trust, patience, boundaries, unconditional love, or myriad other lessons. I invite you to embrace their presence in your life, even if you don't feel you want to embrace them physically. Who knows? When you discover their added purpose in your life, it may become easier to tolerate them. Or not. Either way, you don't have to choose between love and intolerance. They can exist simultaneously. Q

Fear builds physical, mental, and spiritual walls. With so many walls, it's difficult to move about freely in your physical, mental, and spiritual life. Fortunately, love knocks down those walls so we can be free of fear's confinement. I invite you to be a wrecking ball of love. 😲

There is a difference between being a victim of an unfortunate event or circumstance and being a victim of your own thoughts.

May you be a victim of neither. 💭

In anything you read, in anything you hear, or upon any conversation you have, ultimately, the last voice you hear is always your own. The dialogue you have with yourself tells you what you are making it all mean. No words can hurt you or anyone else unless you are telling yourself they are true or untrue. You will believe (or not) based on your inner dialogue.

I invite you to become acutely aware of your inner dialogue, especially if it is negative, if you are prone to beating yourself up, and when you may be unfairly judging others. What are you saying to yourself? What are you believing or not believing that may be holding you back from how you want to feel? It may be time to review your self-communication skills.

Though neither may be the easiest or most convenient in any given situation, self-respect and integrity are always kinder than revenge.

It is said there are only two reliable certainties any of us can claim:

> 1. The reality of our existence.
> 2. The fact that no matter what we believe, we could be wrong.

I invite you to embrace the possibility that you could be wrong—and that's okay. You may even find it to be liberating.

Of course, I could be wrong about that. 📚

Embarrassed. Humiliated. Ashamed.
>   All three uncomfortable.
>   All three unwanted.
>   All three a perception of a loss of dignity or honor.
>   All three socially driven.
>   All three learned emotions.

Somewhere, at some time in your life, somebody told you what was acceptable to them. Instead of experiencing these learned emotions at the mercy of another's judgment (which we all know we have no power over), I invite you to stay in your own business and decide now what is acceptable to you for you.

There is power in unlearning.

The amount and severity of your stresses and "issues" is a direct reflection of how far you have strayed from your true self.

Is it time to come home to you?

Did you ever buy a product that came with a lifetime guarantee and think that it was going to last forever, only to have it break or not perform after a short (or even an extended) amount of time? If so, my guess is that even though it was guaranteed for a lifetime, YOUR life didn't end.

Sure, you may have been inconvenienced. You may have experienced sadness, anger, confusion, disbelief, or regret. Then what did you do? You most likely went through the steps to have it replaced or repaired through the guarantor, you replaced it with something totally different, or you decided not replace it at all. Whichever you chose, you adjusted and moved on. YOUR life did not end. Yes, it was guaranteed to last forever, but it did not. Different from what you planned. Different from what you expected. But your life did not end.

If you feel stuck about making a decision because you want a guarantee that everything is going to work out for you without having to feel pain or regret, I invite you to stop squandering your time. There is no guarantee of that, and if that's what you're waiting for, my hunch is you're already experiencing pain or regret. I invite you to have faith that the Universe is always working in your best and highest good, no matter what YOU have planned. True, it may not go as you expected. And, as you always have, you will adjust and move on.

Of course, I can't guarantee that.

We routinely do the following to provide visual reminders for important tasks so we can more easily prioritize their importance and quickly bring them to our attention:

Make a grocery list when we need something from the store.
Make a to-do list when we have several tasks we want to accomplish.
Mark our calendars when we schedule an appointment or event.
Highlight passages in books and bookmark websites we want to remember.

Why, then, are we often uncomfortable, hesitant, or even resistant to making visual reminders of the following oh-so-very-important things?

What I REALLY WANT in my life
How I want to feel
How I want to show up in the world
What I am grateful for
Who I am and what my
boundaries are

If you haven't already, I invite you to make these visual reminders and/or lists to remind you of who you are and what you really want. Carry them with you on your phone, in your purse, or in wallet and refer to them daily. The more you see them, the more attention you'll give them. Why should you make these reminders? Because sometimes we forget to remember that true happiness comes from being who we really are. And happiness is our true priority. ◎

It's a brand-new day and your canvas is bare. How will you color your world?

Will you paint within the lines?

Will you improvise on the outline?

Will you go totally abstract?

Will you be minimalistic, or will you use all of the colors available to you?

Whichever life-art mode you choose, I invite you to let it flow! Enjoy the reveals and unveiling of each piece you create. Great conversations. Productive energy. Completed tasks. Wisdom gained. Thoughts contemplated. Memories made. Do your best to avoid the pitfalls of drawing the wrong conclusions and painting yourself into a corner!

At the end of your day, step back and take a look. Did you create another masterpiece? If so, great! If not, that's great too. Because either way, every tomorrow you will get another bare canvas, and you will always be the artist who gets to paint it. ⚲

Everything that anyone has ever achieved was achieved because, at some point, no matter how apparent or hidden their belief was, it existed.

If there's something you want to do or be or achieve, I invite you to embrace and repeat this mantra: "It's doable. It's doable. It's doable!"

Imagine how your life would feel if you looked at it from the observed experience point of view and expressed your "I Am-ness" in those terms. For example, "I can see that I'm having an abundant money experience right now" or "I can see that I'm having an uncomfortable work situation experience right now" or "I can see that I'm having an overwhelmed-lack-of-time experience right now" or "I can see that I'm having a proud parent experience right now." Looking at things from an observed experience point of view allows you to step back and put perspective on what's happening now as well as what has happened in the past. You can see how your many, many experiences differ. Some experiences delight you and some don't. Further, you have the understanding and confidence to more easily accept and flow with life's changes, knowing they are merely experiences.

If you're trudging along in the same-old-same-old, feeling like the monotony will never end and just looking for some light at the end of the tunnel, I invite you to remember the "Won't it be great!" game. Think of what it is you really want and envision yourself having it:

Won't it be great when more money comes to me?!

Won't it be great when I'm feeling much healthier?!

Won't it be great when I find that perfect relationship?!

Won't it be great when this task is complete?!

Looking to the end result with excited anticipation will inspire and motivate you to keep going. Don't stop—you're almost there! And won't it be great?!

When something you really, really want doesn't seem to be coming, you have two choices:

1. Go into negative self-talk. Tell yourself you don't deserve it. Nothing good ever happens to you. You never get what you want. Mope around. This negativity will help you avoid disappointment and broken expectation (NOT!)

2. Trust that the Universe is working in your best and highest good. Be in a state of gratitude for all the abundance you already have in your life. Adjust your alignment and be open to receive. Carry on with a sense of positivity, knowing that all timing is Divine. This trust and positivity will help you—well, let's face it—be happier and more likely to receive good in your life!

Call me crazy, but I'm recommending #2. Q

The bad news: you will never succeed in making someone else happy.
The good news: you will never fail at making someone else happy.

They always, always, always choose. And so do you.

It's true. Sometimes you can't control the circumstance or the players. But you can always choose how you act toward or react to the circumstances or the players.

And that always puts you in control.

Do you ever sit down with a novel, non-fiction book, operating manual, or newspaper with the intention of reading only the even pages? I'm going to guess your answer is, "Of course not!" And why not? Because you don't want to miss anything important that could be on the other side of the page. Character traits, plot lines and twists, spiritual answers, next-step instructions, and even the weather await on the other side of the page. Reading only the even pages would create gaps that could leave you feeling unfulfilled, incomplete, unsatisfied, frustrated, or confused. You want the full story so you can fully enjoy, understand, learn, or even prepare for something to come. Reading both sides of the page is the best way to assure success in that process.

As you experience times of feeling unfulfilled, incomplete, unsatisfied, frustrated, or confused, I invite you to remember this book metaphor. When you enter into a conversation or situation in which you have a very set opinion or belief, ask yourself, "Did I look at the other side of this page? What information might I have left in the gap that I avoided or refused to look at? What did I skip over that might complete this story?"

In life, as in reading, I invite you to leave no page unturned. How else will you know if there's a happy ending? Q

When you choose to show up fully, you can't be more than you are in any given moment. I invite you to always choose to show up fully. 🎯

From Marie Kondo's *The Life Changing Magic of Tidying Up* to Elsa from Disney's "Frozen" singing "Let it Go", there's been a lot of instruction to let go of things that no longer bring you joy or serve you. Something to keep in mind as you are letting go is, you are creating space to allow the things that you really want to come to you. If you fill that space with something different (but that still doesn't serve you), you're right back where you started. 🔍

This is a simple reminder that you are an adult. The choices you make today and every day are your own and are in the here and now. You can choose to blame the past for the choices you make today (ie., the way you were raised, what your parents told you, or how you were treated), but when it's all said and done, the choices are still yours. With the exception of revisiting good memories and lessons, there's no need to go back to the past. There's nothing happening there. There are no choices to be made in the past.

What do you want in the here and now? The choices are yours—all yours.

It's not the truth that hurts. The truth is what it is. The truth is the clean reality. What hurts are all the thoughts we have around the truth. It's the rules and expectations and shoulds and shouldn'ts that cause the shame, guilt, anger, and fear we feel about the truth. The pain comes from fighting the reality of the truth and from thinking that the truth should be different from what it is. In actuality, the truth is freedom, because once we accept the truth, we unburden our mind from the battle within us. It's true.

Let's say you have a basket full of beautiful, shiny, delicious apples. Except for one. It's rotten and mushy and moldy and smells awful. It's ruining your pleasure-sense of all the other awesome apples, and you can't get your focus off that one bad apple. You finally remove it and throw it in the garbage where it can't damage the other apples. Now you have nothing but beautiful, shiny, delicious apples to enjoy. Yay! Life is good! Unless you keep going back to look in the garbage.

There's nothing in the garbage that you need. Get it?

Can you be open to the possibility that "loss" and "fear of loss" would not be as painful or cause as much suffering if we would simply remember that people are not possessions and that relationships—including those that are parental, familial, romantic, friendships, professional, and casual—are all merely experiences we have for segments of time with no guarantees of a particular outcome?

If you can be open to the possibility, you may find it easier to give yourself permission to enjoy life more. You have nothing to lose. Q

No matter how much work you put in compared to someone else, no matter what formula you use or how much money you spend or how much you think you deserve it more than they do, it's not always going to look or be equal. Their success is theirs, and your success is totally different. There is no need to compare. There is no competition. If you can take all that energy you've been using to compare and compete and shift it to an energy of gratitude that everyone is succeeding differently, you may just find that your success feels much more exciting and satisfying. And the bonus: things get easier. Q

Which is more important when making a decision: intellect or intuition? Is it better to follow your brain or your heart?

Let me ask you this? Which is more important, your feet or your hands?
When you want to stand, it's your feet. When you want to hold something, it's your hands. So, when you want to stand and hold something, are you frozen in a dilemma over which body part is more important? Of course not. Both are equally important, and they work together naturally, without status, to help you.

We are each blessed with intelligence and intuition. I invite you to let go of the level of importance you place on one versus the other and allow the natural cooperation and flow of the two. When you are open, they work as one. Q

"Don't throw the baby out with the bathwater" is an idiom for avoiding an error in which you throw away something good when trying to get rid of something bad, or in other words, reject the favorable along with the unfavorable. My guess is, if you were actually bathing your baby, it wouldn't cross your mind to throw her out just because she is momentarily sitting in dirty water. You would lift your precious baby out, rinse her off, and then discard the muddied water, right?

Funny how this age-old idiom can be applied to present day. We make quick judgments based on generalizations. We unfriend or reject long-held relationships based on current tensions or differences of opinion. We fail to look at the value of the good parts instead of concluding that if the situation is bad, it must all be bad, and therefore we must rid ourselves of all of it.

If you find that the water is looking a little murky in a current situation or relationship, I invite you to dip your hands in and feel around a little. Make sure you're not about to throw away something precious. It's a lot easier to find clean water than it is to replace a precious baby. Q

If somebody gave you $1,440 with no strings attached, would you be willing to pay them back $5 of it to get the answers to your most pressing questions? What if it were even cheaper than that? What if it were free? Seems like a no-brainer, right?

Every day you are given 1,440 minutes. How often do you allow yourself just five minutes to stop your busy mind, drop in, and connect with your inner wisdom? The answers you are seeking are available to you if you give yourself permission to spend time to open your mind and receive them.

Would it be easier to make decisions if you replaced the word selfish with the word "self-responsible"?

When you look at a six-month-old baby rolling around on a play mat, kicking and squealing with delight, do you see the baby as incomplete because she can't yet walk? In all her evident joy, do you think the baby is feeling incomplete? I'm guessing your answer is NO. I'm also guessing you wouldn't want or expect the baby to be unhappy until the time it can walk. Am I right? Why is it then that we tend to withhold happiness for ourselves until we feel complete? (ie., I'll be happy when I lose this weight, write this book, get this job, find the right mate...)

Here's a little tidbit of information for you: we are all incomplete until we leave the planet. The incompleteness is what keeps us moving forward; it's our constant quest for happiness. And since seeking happiness is the ultimate reason why we do everything we do, why not relax and be happy as much as possible on the journey. You don't have to delay happiness in order to reach a goal. As a matter of fact, withholding happiness ultimately makes goals more challenging to reach. Happiness is available all the time!

I invite you to take a cue from the delighted baby. Be happy now, and trust that you will also be happy later. Happiness is the closest you will ever feel to being complete. Q

What's your plan for all that time you have while you're waiting for things to be perfect?

Just asking.

Imagine standing in line at the grocery store and seeing your picture on the National Inquirer and Star magazine, associated with an enormous red headline that simply isn't true. You're not even a celebrity (or maybe you are!), yet everyone you know shops at this store and will see this! Rumors will fly, and you'll probably feel humiliated, frustrated, betrayed, and helpless as the rumors grow. Sure, you can contact the magazines and demand a retraction, but the damage has been done, and it will be a challenge to undo it. That's how gossip works.

I invite you to remember the value of your truth and have the integrity to value the truth of others before innocently or purposely passing on information that hasn't been validated. Once it's out there, it's out there, and it's so much easier to let the cat out of the bag than it is to put it back in.

Have you ever set a goal or intention for something you really want and then find that you immediately started self-handicapping?

- "I didn't get a lot of sleep last night, so I probably won't be able to..."
- "I really didn't eat that much, so I probably won't..."
- "I had so little time to prepare, so it probably won't be..."

Self-handicapping is a way of lowering your expectations for yourself so you won't be disappointed if you come up short. Self-handicapping is self-sabotage.

If this is a pattern for you, I invite you to review your goal or intention and the reasons you want it; then ditch the excuses. Quit bailing on yourself before you start. Stop preempting a positive outcome with words, and let your actions speak for themselves. Quit trying to protect yourself from failure and defeat, and start putting your energy into embracing the challenge. Be better than your excuses.

Of course, you don't have to. I hear mediocrity is "okay." 🎯

Your beliefs around money determine what's possible for you. If, deep down, you believe it's impossible for you to have plenty of money, then it's pretty close to impossible that plenty of money will come to you, because that belief shuts out the possibility for creativity to allow it into your life.

All those people who you think are "lucky" or "special" are actually people just like you— with a different set of beliefs.

Change your beliefs, change your outcome.

There are plenty of people who will tell you, "Be yourself!" or "You be You!" yet conversely follow it up with spoken or unspoken exceptions or judgments:

- except when in the presence of ...
- except at the location of ...
- except if you are ...
- except if it affects ...
- except if you look like ...

Mostly what they're really saying is, "It's okay with me for you to be you, as long as being you is not a contradiction or inconvenience to me or my agenda."

I invite you to remember that there are no exceptions to who you really are. You get to choose how you navigate the social norms and if, when, or how you want to fit in to anyone else's world. That's being you.

Perhaps the reason so many people are challenged with the idea of meditation is that for so long we've been taught to "do". To "get it done." To "Go! Go! Go!"

Meditation is the state of allowance where, for just a few moments, you stop running the show. You stop trying to make everything happen. It's truly a time where you "BE all you can BE."

What if, for just 15 minutes a day, you allowed yourself to BE instead of DO? You'll never know until you give yourself permission to try.

Anxiety feels like the heightened energy of worry. It's like worrying about something while you're simultaneously worrying that you're worrying about it. It's the product of feeding the fire of fear. The more fuel you put into it, the higher the flame rises, and before you know it, the fire is out of control.

Anxiety is no joke. While it can be extremely challenging, I invite you to remember that you have the power and authority to step outside your anxiety and ask, "What would it feel like if I were not afraid?" Even the slightest reprieve from feeding the flame can reduce the heat.

There are several varieties of grapefruit, yet unless you were a grapefruit expert, chances are you wouldn't be able to tell them apart until you broke them open and looked inside. Once open, you'd see that all were not the same color. You might even find a couple that appeared the same but tasted different. Some would be sweet, and some would be sour. How would you ever know what you preferred if you didn't take the time to look inside?

Life is like a box of grapefruit.

"You can please some of the people all of the time, you can please all of the people some of the time, but you can't please all of the people all of the time."
—*Poet John Lydgate, as made famous by Abraham Lincoln*

You can set an intention to please the most important person all of the time by practicing self-respect, self-love, boundaries, kindness, patience, and integrity.

Hmmmmm. I wonder who that is...

Some of life's greatest injustices happen within the hallowed halls of our own minds, where we're caught between what we've learned to be true and what we deeply feel and believe to be true.

What are you willing to unlearn today?

When inclement weather is forecasted, we usually have time to prepare and decide whether we will take shelter and wait it out or decide it would be better to evacuate our current position and find a safer place. Unfortunately, we're sometimes caught off guard and end up in the middle of the storm. Whether we are caught in the physical rage of the storm or just the inconvenience of it, we are aware that our environment is undergoing change. When the storm ends, we know that clouds could linger, that there could be debris to clean up, and that there may be permanent, irreparable damage to what was once normal.

AND we adjust, AND we rebuild, AND even through the change, we know that the sun will shine again, because we know that's how nature works.

However ominous your current climate may feel, I invite you to remember, after every storm, you will adjust, you will rebuild, and the sun will shine again. Q

Here's a little true or false quiz regarding failure:

> 1. When you give a hungry person money for food and they spend it elsewhere, you have failed as a humanitarian.
> 2. When you give your children guidelines and rules and they don't follow them, you have failed as a parent.
> 3. When you strive to be the perfect candidate for a job and you're not selected, you have failed at your profession.
> 4. When you put yourself out there to befriend another and they ignore or reject you, you have failed at love or friendship.

Answer key: False. False. False. False.

Here's what's true: their choices are not your failures. Ever.

If you're in the habit of blaming yourself for failing to make (or change) another person's choice, you are choosing to spend your life feeling like a failure. Seems a little counterproductive, don't you think?

You have a to-do list a mile long. Places to go. People to see. Deadlines to meet. The world's full of drama. You're trying so hard to make things go right. They're not cooperating. They don't get it. You're frustrated. It's not working. The pressure is building. How do you make it stop?!

Truthfully, some of it won't stop because it's totally out of your hands and some of it you already know how to control—you just have to choose to do it. In the meantime, I invite you to give yourself permission to take just one minute a few times a day, close your eyes, breathe deeply and slowly, and repeat this mantra:

"It's all temporary."

May you capture and embrace the experience of constant change and be grateful for the Power of Now.

Not doing something because one is afraid to fail is basically just failing in advance but without the honor and closure of having at least tried.

When captive monkeys and apes feel threatened, get angry, or are just bored, they often fling their poo to exhibit their emotions, sometime aiming specifically, while other times just "throwing it out there," not knowing or caring what or whom it lands on or who has to clean it up. Humans tend to find this behavior vile and disgusting, yet we often fail to see where we do the same.

Today's world is rife with metaphorical "poo-flinging." I invite you to remember that you are not a captive animal but a human being in charge of your own actions and energy. There are clean and kind ways to express yourself.

If you want to help build a cleaner and kinder world, don't be part of the sh*t show.

Here are four things to do when things are out-of-whack:

> 1. Do what you can to control the things that are yours to control (including thoughts and emotions).
> 2. For all the things that are out of your control, send loving and positive energy that they may come back into balance in Divine timing.
> 3. Help others when you can and if it feels good to do so.
> 4. Keep moving forward with the knowledge that everything will eventually be okay.

Please notice that "worry" is not listed.

There are 24 hours in a day and 365 days in a year. A jar of mayonnaise weighs 30 ounces, 2+2=4, and the US was founded in 1776, making it over 240 years old right now.

Did reading any of these bits of reality make you feel bad in any way? What did you make the information mean? Are you suffering from having read them? My guess is your answer is, "Duh. No."

Now fill in the blanks with your own facts: I am __ years old. I weigh __ pounds. My waistline is ___ inches. I wear size ___. My bank account balance is $___. I owe $___.

Did filling in any of these bits of reality make you feel bad in any way? What did you make the information mean? Are you suffering from having read them? My guess is that at least one of those numbers gave you a negative twinge. You might have even gone into beat up or shame mode. Funny thing is, they're numbers, just like the ones in the first paragraph. Just numbers. Just a measurement. Just the reality of where you are today.

It's not the numbers that hurt. It's your thoughts about the numbers. I invite you to thank the numbers for their truth, which is allowing you to find your truth.

U sually, the answers to your questions will come more quickly and clearly if you ask them with positive energy.

If you are asking a question like, "WHAT AM I SUPPOSED TO DO?!" while feeling panicked, resentful, or afraid, that energy will block you from receiving a clear answer. If you change your energy, take a deep breath, and simply and quietly say, "Please show me what to do," you will open your heart and mind to receive the clear answers you seek.

Isn't it worth a try? Keep calm and ask. 😯

Even the most experienced lifeguards know that a drowning person is the most dangerous type of rescue. In a panic, someone drowning is likely to claw at their rescuer and try to climb to the surface at all costs. There have been many incidents of drowning victims and their would-be rescuers being lost together, especially in muddy or icy water. If the drowning victim is conscious, the best way to rescue them is to stay out of the water and provide them with tools to pull themselves out.

If you encounter someone drowning, I invite you to keep your feet planted firmly on the ground or remain in your own boat and stay calm. You can be of much more help to them if you don't jump in and succumb to the muddy or icy water that surrounds them.

And, yes, this is definitely a metaphor.

Oh, the wonders of investing in modern technology:
instant oatmeal, drive-thru windows, microwave ovens,
cell phones, email, social media, credit cards, and
Netflix. Want it now? You got it! Just pay the man.

Oh, the dividends of investing in heart-based living: lasting
relationships, understanding, trust, deep love, wisdom, true
connection, knowledge, and faith. These take longer. They
last longer. And they pay you.

Invest wisely, my friends. Q

Are you negatively hedging your bets as you work to manifest your dreams?

"This will probably never happen, but I'd love to win the lottery."
"I'm pretty sure he/she doesn't exist, but I'd love to find the perfect partner."
"I'm sure I'm under-qualified, but THAT would be my dream job!"

We do this so we won't be disappointed if we don't receive what we want. Unfortunately, the Universe is going to give you whichever vibe is stronger, so if you're "pretty sure" it's not going to happen, then the Universe says, "Okay, they don't want this to happen. So shall it be."

If you want to manifest your dreams, I invite you to drop the negative precursors. It's much more efficient to say, think, and vibrate the direct positive, like "I'd LOVE to win the lottery!" or "I'd LOVE to find the perfect partner" or "THAT would be my dream job!" Remember to fully want what you want with gusto! It makes the Universe's job so much easier to deliver.

A bullet train, a sailboat, a snowplow, a bicycle, a Rolls Royce, a wheelbarrow, and a kite all leave the station in pursuit of their destination. They all take different routes at different speeds, and they all get there when they get there.

Life's never a "story problem" unless you choose for it to be.

To "respond in kind" means to react to something that someone has done to you by doing the same thing to them. So, for example, If one taunts the other out of anger or frustration, the other would respond with the same "kind" of words. Many times, the exchange escalates to the point that both parties walk away in a cloud of negativity that follows them throughout their day or longer. Who wins, and at what cost?

Wouldn't it be great if we could learn to "respond in kindness" in those situations and deescalate that negative energy? Before you respond in kind to a negative action, I invite you to ask yourself, "What will this response cost me? Is it worth ruining the rest of my day?" You can at least respond in kindness to yourself by committing not to carry the weight of their negative energy.

249

Have you ever had one of those moments where you were pushing-pushing-pushing on a door that wouldn't open, only to look down and finally realize there was a sign that said "Pull"? Or maybe you turned onto a street to see traffic coming straight at you because you forgot to pay attention to the sign that said "One Way"? Or you stood and waited (and waited) at the hostess station at a restaurant because you didn't read the sign that said "Please Seat Yourself"? It can feel frustrating, embarrassing, and just plain foolish when we don't notice these simple, common signs that were there all along. The good news is, once you've felt the negative emotion a time or two from missing the signs, you start to pay a little more attention and actually look for and welcome the signs so you can adjust accordingly before moving forward.

There are so many signs the Universe/God, your body, and your intuition show you every day that can help steer you in the right direction if you'll only start to pay a little more attention to them. When you're tired, sleep. When you're hurting, give yourself time to heal. When someone is pushing your buttons, remember your boundaries and intentions. When you are anxious, take time to center. The signs may not be printed in words that you can read, but you know what they are and what to do. Ignoring them will most likely leave you feeling frustrated, embarrassed, and just plain foolish, so I invite you to remember the good news, adjust accordingly, and keep moving forward.

There will always be someone who tries to steer you with their free advice or opinions, solicited or not. How kind! How generous! And sometimes, how pushy!

I invite you to keep this in mind: even if you asked for advice or an opinion, you are under ZERO obligation to act upon it. You get to choose whether it works for you or not. A sincere and kind response of "Thank you very much. I'll take that under consideration when making my decision" firmly places you in the driver's seat.

Did you know there are three types of tears?
1. The human body produces five to 10 ounces of basal tears each day just to keep our eyes from completely drying out.
2. Reflex tears protect the eye from irritants, such as smoke or onions or strong wind.
3. Emotional tears start in the cerebrum where sadness is registered, then the endocrine system is triggered to release hormones to the ocular area.

All three types are produced as responses. We trust and rely on our body every day to do what it naturally does without constantly questioning how it works. We sneeze, walk, scratch, rest, smile... all in response to what's happening around us without a thought as to how our body is processing it.

Why is it then that we often feel shame with emotional tears when they are just our body's response to what's happening around us? We don't feel shame when we blink, and we don't feel shame when we peel onions. The answer can only be that we've been taught to feel shame. "Big girls/boys don't cry."

I invite you to let your tears flow freely and openly without shame or resistance. Your body knows exactly what it's doing and why without the opinion of anyone else. Some teachings are best unlearned.

Can you have a change of heart? While anything is possible, it may be more likely that you have a change of thought or a change of belief that exposes a deeper layer of your heart's truth and/or true essence. It is not our heart that needs to change. It is our heart that guides us to make change and grow.

If you find yourself overwhelmed or constantly repeating, "I don't have time," be assured that there are a bazillion different ways to get organized or be a better planner. However, all the organizing and planning will NOT give you more time. You already have all the time you need and all the time you're going to get. We all get the same number of hours in a day and days in a week. Uh-oh. Now what?!

I invite you to start by being clear about what you really want, then taking ownership of your time. Don't give it away randomly when your intention is to be focused (even if the focus is on rest or play!). You get to choose how you spend your time just like you choose how you spend your money. If you had limited funds but had to pay a premium price for every social media post, email or text you read, or every TV show that sucked you in, would you be spending your money that way? You choose to be focused or to be distracted. What do you really want?

When you hold on to something very tightly in an effort to control it, the movement of that something becomes restricted. It can no longer bend, flex, grow, flow, give, or receive. And, the part of you that is doing the tight holding is also restricted.

We've been told to hold on tightly to our dreams. Wouldn't it seem more productive to loosen the grip? Dreams need faith and freedom to come true.

Intuition speaks through your body. Sometimes intuition is referred to as a "gut feeling," however that's not necessarily true for everyone. You may feel it in your heart, chest, shoulders, back, ears, head, or anywhere else in your body. It could feel like a tingling, a chill, a vibration, a rumbling, a constriction, or a wave. It may be subtle or overwhelming. No matter where or how you feel it, remember that it's your inner guidance system using your body to alert you to stop and listen. Tune in to your body, and you will tune in to your own wisdom. 🎯

Be strong enough to do what works for you, even if it's not the latest fad, the most popular, or the most efficient approach. If it works for you and you are happy with the results, that's what matters.

At the same time, be honest enough to know when it's not working for you and where you desire different results. Then be open to new ways to make it work so you can be happy. Because that's what matters. 🔵

You can make every effort possible to gain the admiration and respect of other people OR you can be your authentic, honest, and open self and live a life that you admire and respect.

Why would you choose to work so hard when you ultimately know that other people always get to choose whether or not they admire and respect you?

Just a hint if you're still trying to decide how hard to work at it: It seems the thing that people most admire and respect about others is their authenticity, honesty, and openness. Go figure.

I s it possible to take two seemingly unrelated challenges and combine them to create a feel-good solution? Let's experiment with these two variables:

1) the neverending question of "How do I practice self-love and appreciation?" and 2) the toxic energy we hold and emit into the Universe when we negatively express judgment around someone else.

Possible solution: Every time we observe ourselves judging someone negatively, we turn it into self-love and appreciation.

Judgment: That person drives like an idiot!
Self-love appreciation: I'm so glad I'm a considerate driver. I love that about me!

Judgment: That person is fat and lazy.
Self-love appreciation: I'm so glad I'm only responsible for my body and my health. What a relief!

Judgment: That person is so WRONG!
Self-love appreciation: I'm so glad I have the presence and ability to choose what I believe and what's right for me at any time. I love my freedom!

Do you see how turning the judgment into self-love appreciation takes the negative wind right out of the judgment and makes you feel better at the same time? The

toxicity evaporates and the positivity expands! I freaking
LOVE science! By all means, TRY THIS AT HOME! 🔴

It IS all lining up—whatever your "it" happens to be. Let's take a piece of delicious cake, for example. You clearly desire a piece of cake. You order it. The waitress brings it to you. You eat it and you are happy (because it's CAKE, for crying out loud!) But before you were happy eating the cake, all of this (and more) happened:

> • the ground had to be cleared and plowed; and the wheat had to be planted, harvested, processed, packaged, shipped, distributed, received, measured, mixed, and baked (along with the other ingredients that underwent the same process!)
> • the chickens had to be hatched from eggs, raised on a farm that had to be built, then lay eggs that had to be processed, packaged and shipped, distributed, received, etc.
> • the restaurant had to be created from an idea, then built. Chefs and staff had to be hired (who of course all had to be trained beforehand) and recipes developed, not to mention the plates and flatware that were created and processed along with menus, tables, etc.

All this for a piece of cake for you to enjoy! Why am I telling you this? So that when you feel like nothing is happening, or like you are not getting what you want fast enough, or like you are waiting and waiting, you will be reminded that everything IS happening that needs to happen, and it IS all lining up for you—at the right time, in Divine time, you will get IT because you were clear about what you ordered. And, in the meantime, you have the wonderful opportunity to be grateful for everything that is happening behind the scenes to make your dreams come true.

It's happening. 🔍

We use the word "is" to introduce a descriptor or definer of our beliefs about reality. For example, we say things like "the apple is red" or "the sky is cloudy." It helps us go through daily life in sync with the rest of the world and makes it less confusing and more cooperative. Is makes life less complicated—MOST of the time. However, you can fall into an "is trap" when it comes to your thoughts.

If you believe thoughts like "life is hard," "change is hard," "growth is painful," or any other negative thoughts that keep you fearful or stuck, you are defining how your life will be—you're choosing your reality. And when you say it out loud, you're telling others what your reality is too.

I invite you to be open to the possibility that things can be different. Be very selective about your "is" beliefs. Life can be challenging, and life can be joyful. You always have a choice about what you believe. And that IS the truth.

Today IS going to be awesome! 🎨

Instead of spending time conjuring images of everything that could possibly go wrong, why not spend that time conjuring images of everything that could possibly go right?

Now that's conjuring time well spent! 🎯

There is at least one thing you do very well.
     What is it?
There is at least one part of your body that you really like.
     What is it?
There is at least one thing you know better than anyone else.
     What is it?
There is at least one thing that makes you happy every time you think of it.
     What is it?
There is at least one person who cares about you very much.
     Who is it?
If you answered these five questions, you are now looking at evidence that you are valuable, you are worthy, you are capable, you can be happy, and you are loved. How does it serve you to look for evidence to the contrary? 🎯

Vocabulary.com says, "A peeve is an annoyance and a pet peeve is an annoyance that's nurtured like a pet—it's something someone can never resist complaining about. There are all kinds of pet peeves, like littering, misusing punctuation, driving slowly in the fast lane, or talking during movies. If something like that drives you crazy and you have to yap about it, it's a pet peeve. It is an opportunity for complaint that is seldom missed."

We know that complaining lowers our vibration and our ability to manifest the things and feelings we want, so it may be helpful to investigate what we believe we're gaining by complaining about something we can't control in others. If you have a pet peeve, ask yourself: is it an ego thing—a desire to feel superior or right? Is it a rules and beliefs thing, such as "people should or shouldn't do that"? Is it an inconvenience thing, or do I think somebody is taking my time away from me? Is it a need to be heard or acknowledged? The not-so-great news is, whatever the annoyance, it is truly your issue. The great news is you get to choose to keep complaining and refueling a negative vibration or let it go and move toward more positive thoughts.

I know I sound like a broken record here, but this choice thing rocks!

Everyone in your life is here either to teach you or to learn from you, often both. Here are a couple tips if you want to maximize the benefits of all parties involved:

- Be open to the possibility that they are here to teach you—and that you might not immediately recognize the lesson. In fact, it may take years for you to see it.
- Be open to the possibility that they are here to learn from you; for them, the lesson may include what NOT to do. Doesn't matter; just be you.
- Remember that we all have our own paths. When someone enters or leaves your life, it may not be all about you. They will stay until they've gotten what they came for or given what they came to give, no matter how great or small. You may feel angry or confused or sad. Just remember that you affect other people in the same way. Stay on your path.
- Be grateful for each soul that has agreed to teach you or be taught by you. They're all here to help, no matter what it appears or feels like at the time.

No matter how many different paths, we are all on the same journey. Q

Just because you can do it, doesn't mean you have to.

Just because it's offered to you, doesn't mean you have to accept it.

Just because it's free, doesn't mean you need it.

Just because they're family, doesn't mean you're obligated.

Just because they say it's true, doesn't mean you have to believe it.

How do you decide? Ask yourself, "What feels right for ME?" They'll get over it. Or not. Either way, your life remains YOUR life. You always get to choose. Choose what's right for you.

Does your dream feel impossible? Have you exhausted all possibilities for solving a problem? Probably not. Ask yourself these questions:

- Is it possible that the timing is not right for me right now?
- Is it possible that I don't have all the information I need?
- Is it possible that this is not mine to solve or control?
- Is it possible that I'm not open to other possibilities?
- Is it possible that I have lost faith or trust that it can happen?

It seems like the only thing that is impossible is exhausting all the possibilities.

There are two simple but powerful words that can change the course of someone's day, lift their spirits, provide validation, deter negativity, illuminate kindness, present love and project sincere gratitude.

THANK YOU.

How awesome that you get to reap the same benefits when you say it.

The power is in your hands. Use it generously.

Inertia. What is it?

> 1. A tendency to do nothing or to remain unchanged.
> 2. A property of matter by which it continues in its existing state of rest or uniform motion in a straight line, unless that state is changed by an external force, ie, "A ball rolling down hill will continue to roll unless friction or another force stops it."

Inertia sounds safe and easy...until it isn't. The results can be catastrophic.

What's the inertia level in your life? Are you simply going through the motions? Are you letting life happen to you? You can do that—choose to remain unchanged or be inactive in your thoughts and actions and hold hope that the "friction" part doesn't show up in the form of a catastrophe. Or, you can choose to be the force that stops it. Because when nothing changes, nothing changes. Q

It seems the people who make the most excuses also tend to suffer the most regrets.
Funny how things work.

No excuses. No regrets.

While it may be true that someone is attempting to undermine your authority, it is never true that they are taking your power or inner strength. You are the only one who can give that away.

Here's an interesting question for you: If you could change one thing about someone important in your life, why would you? The most common answer is, "because it would make MY life easier." While that may be true, consider this: there's a reason they're in your life, and that is to help you grow. I invite you to take the time to uncover their lesson for you, because it's there.

Easy is nice, but growth is rewarding.

Q: What's the difference between a carpenter who has all the tools he needs to build a house and a carpenter who uses all the tools he needs to build a house?

A: The second builder actually sees his progress.

Be the second carpenter.

When your thoughts are full of shoulds, you engage in a battle with yourself. You believe that things should be different than they are. What you're fighting with is reality.

• I should weigh less than this (reality: you don't)
• I should have more money than this (reality: you don't)
• I should speak up (reality: you don't)

Do you want things to change? I invite you to give up the battle with reality. Quit wasting your time arguing that things should be different. They're not! Once you give up the fight, you free your mind to make choices of how to CHANGE things to what you want them to be.

Hint: when you change should to could, you open the possibility of movement along a better path.

As you make changes in your life and move forward, there will be those who will not be prepared to accept the changes you've made. Most likely, that's because they fear that your changes will affect their life or that they, too, need to make changes that they are not ready or willing to make. That's okay. Keep moving forward. You never have control over their opinions or decisions. They will either accept your changes or they will not.

On the other hand, there will also be others who stand in support of your changes, celebrating and shouting, "It's about time!" I invite you to consider hanging with these people, and of course, keep moving forward.

It's funny how we hang on to some things just in case we need them someday. Like a full set of cocktail glasses, even though we never entertain. Or an old ash tray even though we quit smoking 10 years ago. Or how about those clothes in the closet that are three sizes too small or too big?

None of these things has served us in years, yet we hold on to them just in case we need them in the future. Plus, there's that thought that if we get rid of them, it will look and feel like we don't have anything! Unfortunately, this unnecessary stuff fills space in our homes, leaving us less free to move around and fill the spaces with things that are useful and make us happy.

We do the same with thoughts. We keep them because "Hey, I've always had them; I grew up with them! Sure, it's obvious that they're not serving me, and many of them aren't even true, but I can't let them go. I need to keep them, just in case I don't know what to think in the future. If I don't have these thoughts, I won't have anything to protect me!"

It's time for spring cleaning, my friends. What is no longer serving you, materially, mentally, and spiritually? What have you been holding on to just in case? It's time to clean house.

We live in an abundant world. There is plenty of everything to go around. You can choose to be jealous and resentful of the people who have more than you, but those thoughts won't make them any less rich or make you any richer. They will only shut off your allowance to the flow of abundance that those people have let in.

The happier and more accepting you are of them, the more open to the flow you become.

Go with the flow.

Questions we use when we're struggling: Why is this so hard? Why can't I make this work? Why is it always a struggle?

Better question to ask when we're struggling: What is the easier way?

Easy does it.

When your fuel light comes on, you stop and get gas.
When the traffic light turns yellow, you slow down.
When the railroad crossing flashes red, you stop and wait.
All are danger signals that let you know which choice to make
for your own safety.

The feeling of overwhelm is a danger signal. It's your body's
way of telling you your load is too heavy for your mind
and/or body.

Will you choose to take action for your own safety?

Real faith is letting go of the need or expectation for a
guarantee, and believing and allowing the Universe to
work for your best and highest good.

Have faith.

This is a world of infinite possibilities.

The minute you deem something impossible, it becomes so. Impossible is all in your mind.

Alan Finger lost 100 pounds in one month without surgery because he believed it was possible. True story.

I invite you to let go of the thought, "That's impossible." It's getting in your way. To change your energy, you have to change your thinking.

How would your world change if you opened space for possibility?

It's all possible. 🔍

Sometimes the hardest and scariest thing to do is face and accept your own truth.
Fortunately, it's also one of the most liberating things you'll ever do, and the payoff is well worth the risk. 😲

We know this is a world of infinite possibilities and your imagination is the space where possibilities manifest first and fastest. So why not help the Universe bring you what you want by making a plan?

If you desire more money, have a plan for what you will do with it! Don't be vague and say, "I'll pay my bills." If $5,000 dropped in your lap today, how would you spend it? How about $10,000? What about $20,000? Be specific. When you use your imagination and visualize what you want, you set a vibration for that abundance instead of staying in a vibration of lack.

The Universe fulfills your desires in accordance to your vibration. Why not plan to vibrate abundance? What do you have to lose? 🎯

As you walk the path of change, of getting what you want and feeling the way you want to feel, there will be people in your life who won't understand what you're doing. They're used to your old story. They're comfortable with your misery. They fear losing control of you. They may mock you, be angry with you, try to lay guilt or blame on you, or shut you out of their life.

This will be their choice. Just as you have made the choice to better your life, so can they if they choose. Stay on your path. You have just become the teacher. Q

Y ou are the keeper of your energy whether you choose to accept that responsibility or not. If you're feeling used and taken advantage of, that's on you.

I invite you to begin today by setting loving boundaries for yourself. Speak them out-loud to those who need to hear them, or set them energetically. Write your boundaries down. "This is what I want." "I will no longer tolerate this." "I am not willing to exert myself in that way anymore." Affirm your boundaries to the Universe/God. Ask for strength in your intention.

You don't have to justify them. You don't have to defend them. Just BE them. Set your loving boundaries and stick by them. It will change the way you experience the world. It will change the way you love yourself.

You've probably said, "Hindsight is 20/20" at some point in your life. The question is, are you using the gift of the wisdom you uncovered, or do you keep repeating the same lesson?

When you get that I've-been-here-before feeling, I invite you to look at the past evidence. What did you uncover? What did you learn? What did you change? And more importantly, what didn't you change?

If you didn't use the wisdom of your hindsight this time, a new opportunity will surely present itself and remind you it's time to make a change.

The past. What a teacher!

Whap do I really want? THAT is the question that guides your actions. To make it easier to get what you REALLY want, practice the "Closer or Further Away" game. Ask yourself:

Will this candy/wine/TV show get me closer for further away from the physical health I really want?

Will this web surfing/Facebook viewing/office reorganizing get me closer or further away from creating the business/career/purpose I really want?

Will this spending/gambling/ignoring my finances get me closer or further away from the financial independence that I really want?

Will this not-speaking-up/not-being-honest/not-being-open get me closer or further away from the relationship that I really want?

You get the picture. Now it's your turn.

Money is a neutral thing. It can be proven to exist or not exist. It's a fact. It's a number. It can be a number on paper. It can be a number on your computer screen. It can be a number on a receipt. It can be a number on a dollar bill in your wallet.

This money, this number, doesn't hold any power on its own. It has no emotional charge. It can't create pain, and it can't create pleasure. It's just a number. The only power it has is the power we give it. And we give it power through our stories.

What stories are you telling yourself about money? What power are you giving to the numbers? What are you making them mean?

P.S. The same goes for the number on the bathroom scale or the size tag in your clothes. 🎯

While it is true that technology has changed our lives, it has also changed the expectations of ourselves and others.

I invite you to remember that we are still human. We still need time to process thoughts and give others time to do the same. Just because we CAN answer or respond in the blink of an eye does not mean we are obligated to do so.

Take the time to align with your thoughts and emotions before hurrying to meet the perceived expectations of others. Know your truth. Communicate your truth in your time. The truth is always worth the wait.

There is a big difference between motivation and inspiration.

You have to "get" motivated, which usually means that you have to find an outside reason to do something you feel you should or have to do.

Inspiration comes from within. The word means "in spirit." Inner passion. The part of you that already is.

Motivation is the push. Inspiration is the pull. What inspires you today?

Some people think of acceptance as giving up or surrendering. Acceptance is not submission or surrender. Acceptance is merely acknowledgement of the reality of the situation. After you acknowledge the facts, then you can decide what you're going to do about it. Q

The Universe sends you messages all the time. If you are listening, you will be able to answer this question: what needs my attention today?

Actors and actresses get paid for adding drama to made up stories and call it their job.

The rest of us do it for free and call it our life.

Control is a tricky thing. Sometimes we want to tell the people who are trying to control us to just stop and leave us alone! We want to tell them to mind their own business and let us live our lives! And in those moments, what are we trying to do? Control them. Darn it!

Instead, we could teach them how to stay in their own business and live their own lives by staying in our own business and living our own lives. They get to choose how they will act and what they will think, and so do we.

P.S. Trying to manipulate somebody's feelings is a form of control. Invitation beats manipulation every time. 🎯

Sometimes anxiety hits hard and fast. Sometimes it's anger, or frustration, or humiliation. Sometimes it's depression, fear, or guilt.

Remember that you have the resources and power for instant relief in this very, very short meditation:

Breathe in love.
    Breathe out fear.
Breathe in calmness.
    Breathe out chaos.
Breathe in peace.
    Breathe out pain.
Breathe in light.
    Breathe out darkness.

Rinse and repeat as needed.

Since the beginning of time, one year has followed the next. Within the year, each month has fallen in order. As has each week, each day, each minute, and each second. Since the beginning of time.

Just as we unconsciously trust that there will be air for the next breath we take, we can trust that we have all the time we need. And the biggest blessing of all...we get to choose how we exist in its infinity.

When you're feeling overwhelmed, hurried, even panicked that you won't get it all done, or when you're frantically saying, "I don't have time for this!" I invite you to look at the overwhelming evidence. The air is always there. The next second/minute/week/month/year continues to be there. Since the beginning of time.

Panic or trust. Which feels better? 😮

There are 3 simple steps to get what you really want:

1. Ask for it! Do you want more money? Ask for it! Better health? Ask for it! A loving and fulfilling relationship? Ask for it!

2. Believe. Believe that you deserve it. Believe that you are worthy of it. Believe that it is on its way, effortlessly, to you. Believe that it is yours to be had. Let go of all doubts and worn-out beliefs.

3. Receive. Be open to receiving what you asked for. Let go of "how" it's going to get here. Let go of control of when it's going to get here. And, when it arrives, receive it with an open and grateful heart.

Ask. Believe. Receive. 🎯

Have you ever been stuck in the fear of starting? You might fear that the task at hand may be overwhelming, or that it will take too much time, or that you won't finish, yet you forget to consider the time you're wasting by sitting in your fear of starting. Or, you fear that you will make a mistake or wrong decision along the way when you haven't even started the process.

If you're stuck because you afraid to start, I invite you to take a deep breath, get out of your head, and start exactly where you are. Start in the middle, start at either end; start with one word, one step, one bite, one stroke of the brush. Just start. There can be no finish without the start. Once you're in motion, the path to the finish will be shown. 😮

There is no wrong way. There are only longer and more challenging lessons. 💭

Fear is what we experience in the face of immediate danger, like a tiger appearing before you out of nowhere. Worry is what we experience when we start predicting what could happen. Even in the case of the tiger, once the initial fear is felt, we immediately indulge our thoughts in worry. "Will he eat me?" "How will I escape?" They are all thoughts set in the future, and yet nothing is happening in the future. It's all happening right now.

Think about it. What are your greatest fears? I would bet the farm that your fears are actually worry about what could or might happen in the future, not immediate danger.

When you feel fearful, I invite you to breathe, center yourself, and ask, "Is there a tiger in my face? No? Then it must be worry, which means it is not happening right now. I'm safe from danger. There is nothing to fear. And then, move forward from this safe place of calm. 😮

Sometimes other people will take it upon themselves to tell you how you should or shouldn't feel.

"You should just be happy you have a partner."
"You shouldn't feel disappointed that you didn't get the part."
"You shouldn't be angry with him; he was just doing his job."

Funny thing is, you DO feel the way you feel! When you suppress how you really feel or force yourself into falsely feeling differently, it often triggers a plethora of other feelings—shame, guilt, anger, self-doubt, depression...shall I go on?

Nobody but you can know how you should or shouldn't feel. Nobody but you feels exactly how you feel. Nobody but you can decide to change how you feel. Nobody but You. You. You.

I invite you to feel how you really feel. Then YOU decide if you want to feel differently. And while we're on the subject, remember that THEY get to feel how they feel too.

In June of 2013, TV cameras recorded Nik Wallenda performing a tightrope walk over The Little Colorado River Gorge in the Grand Canyon on a two-inch wire, 1,500 feet above the water. How does one complete such a stressful and death-defying feat?

He was cognizant of where he was placing his feet.

He grounded himself, connecting and centering with each step.

He prayed, praised and gave gratitude to his God the entire way.

My guess is you don't have plans to cross the Grand Canyon on a two-inch wire anytime in the immediate future. However, you will most likely have days in which it feels you are walking a stressful tightrope. On those days, I invite you to channel your inner-Wallenda. Be aware of where you're going and what you're doing, connect and center yourself with each step you take, and pray and give gratitude to God/Spirit/Universe. Your journey may not be recorded on national television, but your results will feel just as amazing.

INDEX

Choice: 13, 15, 18, 32, 36, 41, 44, 47, 48, 53, 55, 58, 62, 68, 72, 80, 89, 95, 99, 104, 114, 118, 120, 121, 126, 129, 131, 134, 144, 147, 149, 151, 155, 159, 163, 164, 171, 174, 186, 193, 197, 199, 208, 222, 225, 240, 251, 266, 275

Fear: 5, 6, 11, 12, 15, 22, 26, 34, 36, 49, 59, 63, 88, 97, 100, 101, 122, 125, 129, 133, 138, 145, 146, 152, 158, 160, 167, 172, 174, 175, 176, 191, 195, 202, 212, 245, 276, 288, 290, 291

Acknowledgements

My sincerest apologies to the authors of all of the books I've read and admittedly skipped over the Acknowledgements section. In retrospect, I simply didn't understand the complexity and enormity of tasks and people involved in writing and publishing a book. Much more than just sitting down and keeping my butt in the chair to write, the making of this book involved many people and entities, some of whom I've known since childhood. I wholeheartedly invite you to read these Acknowledgements, as the people mentioned are truly praiseworthy, beautiful humans and deserving of much recognition and thanks.

This book exists as a direct result of Deborah Edwards's encouragement and support of Core Living. Deborah has been a critical catalyst of my success and growth, and much more importantly, a loving soul sister and dear friend. My gratitude to Deborah is immeasurable, as is my love for her.

The exploration of my spiritual journey began with my beloved friend, Sue Lindmeier, who opened my eyes (all three of them) and guided me to a life far beyond the realm of religion, and who taught me the power of gratitude, generosity, and kindness. I am forever grateful for her humor, her love, and her true, deep friendship.

I wish every writer could be blessed with an editor as outstanding, as easy to work with, and as hysterically funny as Elizabeth Lyons. Her guidance, enthusiasm, and expertise made finishing this book feel painless and fun. Who says that about writing a book?! Thank you, Elizabeth. May you be ever-caffeinated.

Thank you to Jodi Lustig, who relentlessly (and I'm talking years!) requested (aka hounded me) that I put my Daily Seeds into a book. I did it, Jodi!

To all of my Martha Beck coach cohorts (of which there are *way* too many to mention individually; I would surely leave someone out and feel terrible), to Martha, to my Core Living ladies, and to my awesome clients, thank you for being such a wealth of knowledge and support as well as a most integral part of my journey. I think there will be whole different book about that.

Eternal gratitude to my spirit guides, who meet me willingly on this earthly playground. No other words need to be said aloud.

Finally, I want to thank Brent, whose constant love and support of the real me is sincerely overwhelming every day. Everyone needs a Brent. You are truly worthy of the title "Husband of the Century." To my sons, Blake and Aiden, thank you for your love and patience and daily entertainment. You take the term "never a dull moment" to new heights. And to my "seester," PJ, I'd be lost without you.

About the Author

For over a decade, Sheila Whittington has combined her talents as a Master Life Coach and her well-developed intuition to help others grow and create positive change in their lives. Using her natural gift of connecting with spirit guides and Universal wisdom, she began channeling and translating short teachings into everyday verbiage that we could easily understand and embrace. Started in 2013 for a small but significant group, The Daily Seed is now emailed and Tweeted (@sheilawhitt) to an exponentially growing list of followers across the globe.

Sheila lives in Scottsdale, Arizona with her husband Brent and her sons Blake and Aiden. She offers life coaching and relationship coaching to clients worldwide. She is also a coach for Collective Gain and a Master Coach Instructor for Martha Beck, Inc.

www.SheilaWhittington.com

Made in the USA
Las Vegas, NV
26 February 2021

18624393R00177